PRAISE

Many teachers are creating diverse, equitable and inclusive spaces that welcome and honor students and families. These spaces are created intentionally and, in this book, Hill and Rudnesky share practical, actionable strategies that teachers can implement immediately. This book is for all educators who are passionate about creating and nurturing caring, supportive, and culturally responsive classrooms.

Paul Forbes
Former Executive Director of Educational Equity, Anti-Bias and
Diversity, NYC DOE
Founder of Leading with Hearts and Minds

There is a worldwide battle for the hearts, minds, and souls of the next generation going on as we speak, and teachers have been and always will be the greatest warriors in this fight. This book arms teachers with a good balance of practical knowledge and techniques, along with the wisdom of great thinkers and the personal experience of two *fired up* educators who are on a noble mission. This book is a powerful and important read for both the newest and the most experienced members of the profession.

Joseph Pegues, MA/MED

In *Fired Up Teachership*, Michele and Frank offer practical ways to help you grow as an educator and leader in the classroom. Their strategies will help keep your passion stirred while making an impact on the lives of your students.

Dr. Brad Johnson
Inspirational Speaker
Author of Dear Teacher

Through stories, ideas, and reflections, Frank and Michele inspire us to stay *fired up* and to bring passion to our work each day! They have created a blueprint to develop and embrace the leader that lives in each of us without leaving the teacher behind because, as the reader learns, great leaders are teachers! This is book is real, refreshing and inspirational! Frank and Michele share a message of how we can find joy in teaching, leading, and how each of us can be a difference-maker.

Dr. Evan Robb
Principal of Johnson-Williams Middle School
Author of The Principal's Leadership Sourcebook: Practices, Tools, and Strategies for Building a Thriving School Community and The Ten-Minute Principal

This book is a primer for those entering the teaching profession and a set point adjustment for seasoned educators. It captures the key epistemology of teaching based on a deep personal reflection of seasoned educators and professionals who personify the tenets of the book. It is a practical walk, inspirational in nature, and an effective tool to reflect upon professional and personal practice to be *fired up* each and every day and to be the very best each day for every student in the classroom. The book deserves to be revisited throughout the journey called *Teachership*.

Dr. Christopher Nagy
Superintendent
Educational Futurist and Content Creator

What a wonderful treasure this book is! It is a reminder of the gifts we, as teachers, start every day with, and the opportunities we have to impact. Although there are many factors out of our control, there really are so many things that we do have control of. Both Frank and Michele share such beautiful, diverse, and inspiring stories and so much to reflect upon. This book had me looking inward and searching for ways to not only strengthen my practice, but also for ways to lead by example. Whether you are a first year teacher or a teacher with 27 years of experience, like me, you will be *fired up* about the profession!

Jennifer Lee Quattrucci
M.Ed Education Leadership
Author of Educate the Heart: Screen-Free Activities for PreK-6 to Inspire Authentic Learning

Fired Up Teachership is an inferno! Dr. Frank Rudnesky and Michele Rispo Hill offer a roadmap to not only becoming a more balanced influential leader no matter your position, but does so in a step by step fashion so that the reader understands the bigger picture and is provided the tools to take inspired action! Starting with defining a passion that builds into the legacy you desire, Frank and Michele have filled these pages with *Points to Ponder*, personal anecdotes, and questions on which to reflect. If you are looking to level up by examining every aspect of your leadership from culturally responsive instructional spaces to community involvement you need to read this book. They not only say that "one of the biggest forms of identity theft is telling someone they cannot accomplish something," but breathe life into the opposite by providing the means to achieve a level of servant and transformational leadership to which many strive.

Dr. Christopher Jones
High School Principal | Author | Speaker
Vice-President State Administrator Association

IV

Do you need a spark of encouragement, support, and relevant technique to rekindle your passion for education? In reading the pages of this inspiring book you will ignite your fire within! You will be reminded why you are in education and how you significantly impact and inspire others as well. "....your attitude can be the single most important variable that determines your success as a teacher..." Rudnesky and Hill help you *Fire Up* that attitude and ignite your passions so you are ready to impact your students, your community, and the globe!

Julie Woodard
Artist | Educator | Author

Fired Up Teachership really gets to the heart and soul of the why and what of teaching! With veteran expert educators, Hill and Rudnesky share tales from actual practice and anecdotes from real scenarios that fire up the reader to contemplate and ponder their situations and their reactions. Part autobiographical accounts of a life devoted to education and part a primer for self reflection and personal improvement, this is a great addition to the professional bookshelf!

Michael Lubelfeld, Ed.D.
Superintendent of Schools
Author of The Unfinished Leader, The Unlearning Leader and Student Voice

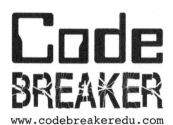

www.codebreakeredu.com

This book is dedicated to the unwavering support and love from my children (Zack, Victoria, Julia, and Jennifer), my husband, John, and my family. They were my biggest cheerleaders to a passionate life in education! This book was made possible by my students, who allowed me to be a special part of their journey, and to my administrators and colleagues who taught me the important lessons of leadership and life.
This book is for each of you. Thank you!
Michele

This is for the people. To my friends and family that saw something in me that I may never have seen. To you who have never met me but we shared a common vision and commitment to disrupt the status quo in a positive light. You made me smile, and my smile lit the flame that stoked the fire that woke the passion in other people.
Thank you! It's never over.
And forever Kim, Franki, Danica. Peace and love always win!
Frank

FIRED UP
TEACHERSHIP

MICHELE RISPO HILL
DR. FRANK RUDNESKY

ACKNOWLEDGEMENTS

It's no secret that we are on the precipice of a massive teacher shortage. It's like a three-legged stool. The first leg is not enough candidates. Many college students are just not choosing to major in education due to many factors including, but not limited to salary, public perception, loss of pensions, and benefits. The pipeline from college to teaching is running dry. The second leg of the teacher shortage stool is that many educators are leaving the field within the first five years of entering the profession for many of the same reasons that people are choosing not to enter the profession in the first place. And the last leg of the shaky stool is that we have a record number of baby boomers and Generation X educators who are getting ready to retire. All of this spells trouble. We are headed for a crisis in filling classrooms with qualified and passionate teachers - and it's why we decided to write this book. While we cannot fix all of these issues that are exacerbating the teacher shortage, we can certainly suggest ways to impact each of these issues by impacting educators like you and pre-service educators. We want to ensure that the next generation of students have the privilege of incredible and passionate educators. We want to support educators, like you, to stay *fired up* throughout your career and positively impact your students.

When people ask me about my career as a teacher, I light up. Truly, I think you might see the glow from my body! I couldn't imagine what my life would be like if I had not become a teacher. In my eyes, it doesn't get any better than this! Teachers make all other professions possible. From the bottom of my heart, I want to say thank you for doing what you do, each and every day. You make me proud!

FMy path in life, leadership, and education has been a storied journey. Like a lot of educators, I did not take a conventional route. Because of this, I have different paradigms from which I view teachership. I acknowledge all the people that found education as their calling. Educators with passion, inspiration, integrity, kindness, respect, gratitude, creativity, strength, love, commitment, and fun: you are the heroes that create heroes. Your legacy begins today. Thank you! Peace and love always win.

TABLE OF CONTENTS

FOREWORD

When Michele gave me a copy of this book, I instantly made a connection with the title. As a long-time educator, I believe that there are two things we can control, attitude and effort. I also understand the challenges that educators face and that we are losing teachers too soon. Some teachers are leaving the profession after only a few years, and some are experiencing burnout, trapped in a career that they can't leave even though they've lost their passion and excitement for their calling. Knowing Michele personally, I knew that her contagious positive attitude would be felt throughout the book, and I read it with the expectation that it would change myself and others for the better. *Fired Up Teachership* is focused on reigniting passion, keeping the fire stoked, and strategies and insights that help educators navigate the highs and lows.

One of the things I like most about the book is that the authors speak honestly from a multitude of experiences, and they share true stories that could have led them to lose their passion. Instead, they both chose to learn from their experiences and keep their fire going strong. Michele and Frank provide real, accessible, and practical lessons for their readers. A positive attitude can be learned, and the authors model this for us throughout this book.

I hope you enjoy this book as much as I did and that it gives you what you need - either a spark, if your flame is fading, or a stoke if your fire is just starting or continuing to be strong. We will all be changed for the better after reading *Fired Up Teachership*.

Jennifer Hogan
Author of The Handbook for Courageous Leadership

INTRODUCTION
IT ALL STARTS WITH YOU

*"I wish people understood that educators are everything to their children.
They are our ancestors' wildest dreams because they are giving children the
building blocks and knowledge to be great."*
K. Carey

Imagine being able to start every day with many gifts. Your
most precious gifts in your role as a teacher are sitting in your
classroom. They are the reason that you come to work every
day. Your students are depending on you to bring the magic,
the sparks— and your passion as an educator.

If your students feel your love and passion, they will respond
in ways that will ignite change in their perception of the world.
It is the first step to becoming a great *Fired Up Teacher*. As you
start your journey or continue on your path, you have to make
a choice. Do you just want to teach or do you want to pursue a
path to *Fired Up Teachership*?

Teachership is not a moment, it's a movement. It's the ability
of a teacher to embrace the leader that lives within them
without leaving teaching behind. It allows a passionate
educator to have the best of both worlds by leading in and out
of the classroom. Teachership is not a position or a title, heck
it may not even be a word that you can find in a dictionary. It's
the mindset of reaching your highest potential as an educator.
It's about digging deep into your soul and finding the very best
teacher you can be for your students and yourself, and calling
them to come forward. Teachership is a choice, one that needs
to be made each and every day. The teacher-leader that you

are, or will become, will profoundly impact your life and the lives of your students. The choice to become a teacher-leader begins with you.

Everyone's path into education is a personal journey, however, there is no doubt that many of your teachers had a great influence on who you became. Some educators sentimentally recall that they wanted to be a teacher from the time they were young children. Others were inspired by teachers that planted that passion. Some may have experienced a life-defining moment that led them into education. While others may have changed career pathways completely and entered education later in life. Whatever the circumstances that led you into education, the important thing is that you are here! Now, your journey as an educator is mostly dependent on one person, you.

YOU ONLY HAVE CONTROL OVER THREE THINGS IN YOUR LIFE: THE THOUGHTS YOU THINK, THE IMAGES YOU VISUALIZE, AND THE ACTIONS YOU TAKE. — JACK CANFIELD

There are a million and one decisions out of your control as a teacher. You don't get to set the hours for your school day, you don't get to choose the students in your class, you may not get to choose the specific curriculum or level that you teach, and so on and so forth. We get it! These are external forces. Those decisions have been made for you. This can be frustrating. While procedures and protocol can certainly impact your role as a teacher, you do have choices. You get to choose your attitude and your mindset, your role as a leader, how deeply you pursue your personal and professional development, and of course, your relationships with your students. This creates endless possibilities for *Fired Up Teachership*.

In your repertoire, your attitude can be the single most important variable that determines your success as a teacher. How you greet the day when you open your eyes in the morning matters. Waking up with gratitude has shown tremendous benefits to your overall well-being, and it will play a huge part in how you interact with others, namely your students, colleagues, and administrators. How do you start your morning?

F When my feet hit the floor, it's a personal victory. I have gratitude for what I had, what I have, and for everything that I am about to have. It gets me *fired up* to anticipate a great day. I do not always have a phenomenal day but happiness is always the goal. I will have unhappy moments and unhappy days but true joy is what I pursue.

That same need for happiness is felt by your students. There will never be a secret formula. However, you can control certain variables. Positive attitudes and affirmations are catchy just like negative vibes. This, you can control. People will feel you.

M The moment that my eyes open, I pause and remind myself how fortunate I am for so many things. I decide that it will be a great day before I get out of bed—and it usually is. With over 30 years of classroom teaching experience, I can tell you that many days are filled with challenges from students, colleagues, facilities, technology issues, and bosses, but there is no more rewarding profession where you can help students discover the best possible version of themselves, and in the meantime, being the best possible version of you. I want you to feel that with every fiber of your being!

People that are more passionate about their vocation will be more likely to go that extra mile for the success of their students. They will find better ways. They will make their students feel safe and loved. They will create a positive climate and culture. You do whatever it takes to connect your students to find their passion. They are truly remarkable at showing you who they are. Think about that. You have that ability to change the trajectory of a student in a positive way. You may already know that, in fact it is why most educators become teachers. Someone inspired them, igniting an interest in a subject, cared for them, and loved them. If you ask them about their favorite teacher, they will likely regale you with stories of a teacher making them feel special, going the distance for them and imparting wisdom, none of which is easily measured in data, but the impact is undeniable! In Chapter 1, we will dive deep into recognizing your "why" that will generate an understanding of how important your role as an educator is to your students —and you.

PASSION BEATS DATA EVERY TIME

This does not mean that data is unimportant. It is another part of your teaching toolbox. There is a plethora of quantitative data that can be accumulated and correlated to variables that can predict outcomes. There are also variables that cannot be measured accurately that will forever impact the future of your students and colleagues.

All mandated qualifications aside, the number one quality of a new teacher hire for us was always passion. You can feel it. You can see it. It can inspire a room. It can inspire a future. The reality is that curriculum and pedagogy can be taught and learned, but passion? It can make an average educator a superstar!

FWhen I was in first grade, our teacher told us that someday by the grace of God, we would find our vocation. We had no idea what she was talking about. That conversation stayed with me all of these years. Believe it or not, education was not my first choice out of the University of San Francisco.

I worked my way through college with financial aid, scholarships, and working in a magic shop while performing magic on the street. I set goals, made a plan, and pointed my compass in a direction. Upon graduation, I moved back to New Jersey and opened a magic shop on the boardwalk in Wildwood, New Jersey.

I studied the art of magic and researched my favorite magicians. Magic became a passion, and I proceeded accordingly with the will to succeed. Although the magic shop was not lucrative in the long run, it was a creative risk that ended with a Houdini act. I was handcuffed, chained up, nailed in a box, and thrown in a river. (Yes, as part of the escape act.) Although magic no longer supports my financial obligations, it will always be a passion. I still practice and perform.

That path is how I found my calling as an educator. The magic shop was closed in the winter. I began to substitute teach. A chance conversation with a principal swayed me to my vocation: education. That is what my first grade teacher was talking about! Your vocation is your calling. It is where you will make the biggest difference in the people around you and the world.

I became a teacher, principal, professor, and now author, speaker, consultant, coach, and disruptor. Along the journey, I added a masters and doctorate degree. Education and leadership became passions.

MI always loved babies and kids. From the time that I can remember, I loved playing house and school. I loved the idea of taking care of little humans and teaching them how to do things to grow and learn. Maybe that's why I had four children of my own! I was a teacher in training from a very young age, but that didn't mean I was a naturally gifted learner. As I moved through my own journey of being a student, I struggled with reading comprehension and grasping advanced concepts in math. I had ADHD (a diagnosis that little was known about at that time) and school was a bit of a challenge for me. With tenacity and persistence, I was determined to graduate from high school and attend college because I would be the first child in my immediate family and the first female in my extended family to attend college. I was eager to make my mark on the world, but I wasn't quite sure of how to do that. It was during my first year at university that I decided that I wanted to make a difference and become a special education teacher to help students like me and so many others. I wanted to ensure that every student that walked into my classroom felt a strong sense of belonging, believed that they could be successful, and would be loved and supported no matter what. That was my promise to my students, and today, it is my legacy.

It feels good to know that you played an important part in someone's journey to awesomeness. It is a privilege and honor to participate in the lives of your students in a meaningful way. It's what fires me up to this day!

Teachership is a journey for you to create a life-long legacy of being a change-maker for your students, your colleagues, and your school. *Fired Up Teachership* will give you practical ways that you can make the leap from ordinary to extraordinary without losing your passion for education and still have balance in your personal life. This book will give you teaching and leadership hacks, from the perspective of a teacher and administrator, that can make the difference in helping the inner teacher-leader in you to step forward and embrace teacher greatness. It's never too late to understand and embrace your role as an educator but it is never too early, either. Come on! Jump in!

We need more educators to disrupt the status quo to create teaching and learning opportunities for our students to see, not only who they are, but who they can become. You may, or may not, have taken a traditional route to life as an educator but something burned inside. Something sparked you to want to make a difference in the lives of students. Whatever it was, we are so glad that you followed your passion to become an educator. We are happy that you are here. We are thrilled that you are ready to take the next step to dive into teachership with both feet!

We hope this book will inspire you and get you *fired up*. The book is divided into four important domains that will help you succeed and excel as an educator. The domains focus on your personal and professional well-being, building connections, the importance of developing routines and procedures, and making an impact. Some days it will not be easy, that's for sure, but trust us, it will be worth it.

Every challenge you face and every opportunity that you are given has a purpose—and it all starts with you! Are you ready?

POINTS TO PONDER
- What is your purpose on this earth?
- How much control do you have on your life?
- Who was your favorite teacher? Why?
- Name ten things that make you happy.

DOMAIN ONE
KNOW YOURSELF

CHAPTER ONE

KNOW YOUR WHY: WHAT GETS YOU FIRED UP?

"He who has a why can endure any how."
Frederick Nietzche

If you have experienced a major crisis in your life, you would have likely had to dig deep and discover things about yourself that you may not have been aware of, or you weren't ready to accept. You certainly would have had to become resourceful and focused to overcome the challenge set in front of you. Your focus was laser sharp and you tapped into energy and potential that you didn't know existed until that very moment. What can often come from challenges is the discovering or rediscovering of your "why" or at least one them. That's not to say that the only way to know your "why" is to be challenged with a crisis. Some people are blessed to have a clear vision of what inspires and excites them from an early age, but many people need to experience life in all of its ebbs and flows to uncover their "why".

So what's the big deal about knowing your "why"? German philosopher Frederick Nietzsche once said, "He who has a why can endure any how." Your why is what sustains you in tough times. It's your north star. It is the constant reminder of what is important to you and the justification of the many sacrifices that you will make in your lifetime. Leadership expert Simon Sinek calls this "the golden circle." He says that it's not enough to know what you do and how you do it. We, at our core, are motivated by why we do what we do.

Of course, people are likely to have more than one "why". If you have a significant other, they may be why you get up every day. If you are a parent, you don't even blink, your children are one of the important "whys" you will have. Families certainly are an inspiration for us to reach for the stars. But what we are referring to in this chapter is your "why" as an educator. Stop and take a minute to jot down the reasons that you became a teacher in the first place.

Most educators can pinpoint the reason that they wanted to become an educator. Passionate educators come alive when they talk about their students; it's palpable. Honestly, our hearts beat a little faster and our smiles widen as we tell you all about our students. Why? Because they are first and foremost the #1 "why" we got into education. If you are in a hurry, don't ask a teacher about their students because you are bound to be there for a while. We both felt a very strong pull to enter a field where we could help students grow and learn, and more importantly, become good people. That is our greatest hope.

Identifying your "why" is as simple as asking yourself the following questions:

1. What do we do?
2. How do we do it?
3. For whom do we do it?
4. Why do we do it? What value are we bringing?
5. What will be my legacy as a teacher?

It's important to note that many people can do the same job, but why they do it will vary, and that's what makes all the difference. Those who recognize their students' best interest as their "why" stand head and shoulders above the rest.

I am very fortunate for all my experiences in school, but most grateful for Mrs. Hill. She taught me things just by being herself even when she didn't know she was teaching. Her affect on me will last forever. She inspired me to become a teacher, and I cannot wait to be on the other side of feeling that way. I want to be a role model for every student that I will have, and I hope to learn from them as well. - Parker

Meet Marge, teacher of English—and so much more. I was fortunate to have Marge as my informal mentor when I first started teaching. Back then, we didn't have a formalized mentor program, so we relied on the kindness of others. Marge greeted me with the biggest smile and assured me that she was there to help in any way she could. She went out of her way to make me feel welcome. Marge checked in with me daily, assisted me with writing lesson plans, helped me program for my students, and taught me everything I needed to know about classroom management. Marge was an awesome mentor, but that was just one of the hats that she wore each day. She was also a member of various committees around the school that helped shape the school's culture. She even found time to show up at the extra-curricular activities and events to support our students. Marge knew that everything was hinged upon the relationships that you built with people. Ask anyone in the school community and they would tell you that they knew that Marge loved her students and was dedicated to her profession. How? It was unmistakable; it was evident in everything that she did! Thank goodness that schools are filled with educators like Marge—people who have come to recognize why they get up every morning and come to school to share their best selves with their colleagues and students. Those are the people you want to follow. They are the people that, no doubt, know their purpose.

Your "why" is personal, but don't believe for a moment that other people do not recognize it when they see it, or more profoundly, when they do not see it. Your dedication to your students and school community communicates what drives you as an educator. It's observable by everyone who is paying close enough attention and it is talked about when members of the community come together or students gather. Parents, students, administrators, and the school community can identify the educators who exude positive energy for their profession. They recognize that your mission is to make a difference with your students and in your school community. Never forget that!

FJust like many educators, my former student Kara took somewhat of a non-traditional route to teaching. During her middle school years, Kara was always drawn towards servant leadership and connecting people in our school. She could often be found helping some of our exceptional students adjust to social and emotional situations around our campus. As her former principal, I am proud to say she exemplified the persona of our community and our school mission: We inspire life long learners and leaders.

At the end of her eighth-grade year, Kara developed a chronic illness that went misdiagnosed for a period of time. In high school, she had to go on homebound instruction until her autoimmune disease was under control. High school years can be riddled with barriers for everyone as you decide your path in life. Add in chronic illness and some tasks may seem astronomical. With support and perseverance, she overcame these challenges and used her positive attitude to find her direction.

Kara went on to achieve an undergraduate degree in liberal arts with minors in English and Irish studies from Villanova University. She had many positive experiences at the college level including service internships that connected her to the community. Although she was always drawn to teaching, external forces kept steering her away from the profession. She tried to make everything else work, except education.

She started to substitute teach. Her first day was in third grade with thirty rambunctious students. At the end of the day, she felt like she got run over by a train but she loved it. Her passion emerged and started changing her future and perception.

When Kara was looking for a masters program in teaching, she reached out to some of her former educators. I was absolutely thrilled that she sought my advice to become a teacher. Education needs her! Her impact has no limits. She will become a master educator.

Ironically, she did her student teaching in the same third grade class where she was a student. Her experience was what she made of it: amazing! Kara is finally at peace with her career choice. With her autoimmune barriers, she does not know if she would have been able to endure the rigors of student teaching along with the challenges of the New Jersey certification process in the beginning of her collegiate career. Now, she sees the end game.

With the strategies she acquired, Kara has been able to persevere in a positive way. I am proud to know her and to reflect on her as that same middle school student that was filled with joy and smiles, and a host of leadership qualities.

She said her experience as a middle school student was one of the catalysts that propelled her into education. Her empathy and understanding have already influenced the type of teacher she hopes to become. She realizes the responsibility of building meaningful relationships and maintaining the endless possibilities that education brings.

Her passion and perspective allow me to see the future of education in a positive light.

I asked, "What will keep you in teaching? We need you."

She replied, "I know I am a new teacher with rose-colored glasses but I am happy and grateful to enter my calling. I will journal, write down my experiences, and reflect. Know your 'why'."

She knows her "why"!

Being a teacher is about sharing your strengths with others and hoping to inspire them in a positive way. It's about doing good work with a sense of purpose and it's about your legacy and how you will measure your life. What impact will you have had on other educators and most importantly, your students? This is your "why"! You may wonder if teaching and education is truly your "why" and that's okay. The future is unknown; we cannot predict what will happen, but what we can tell you is that if you got into the teaching profession for all of the right reasons, it's a great start to a long career. That's what this book is all about—keeping you *fired up* for as long as you serve your students and your school. In times of doubt or when you're feeling overwhelmed, remember to dig deep and remember why you wanted to become a teacher in the first place. Throughout your career, you may have to do this time and time again, but trust that if you center yourself and focus on what you wanted your career as a teacher to be, you'll find your way back to your purpose as an educator.

POINTS TO PONDER

- If you didn't become a teacher, what would have you chosen to do?
- Why are you happy that you didn't follow that path?
- What do you hope that your students say about you long after they leave your school?
- How will you measure your life?

THE FOUR STAGES OF TEACHING

"Love what you teach, but love who you teach more!"
Brad Johnson

A very wise man once said that there are seasons in life, and each season brings new opportunities, challenges, and growth. In these seasons, we learn, grow, and stretch to hone our craft and hopefully become a master teacher. All teachers will move through stages, sometimes multiple times through their career, given life changes and professional changes. Some may move quicker than others to arrive at the master teacher level, and some may never reach the pinnacle of being a great teacher, but we are confident that you will.

FANTASY STAGE

Do you remember fantasizing as a teenager about how great it would be when you turned 18? You would be officially an adult! You wouldn't have to listen to your parents because you were considered an adult by the law. You could stay out all night. You could buy your own car and sign on the dotted line for a loan. The world would be your oyster and you just couldn't wait! Then you celebrated your 18th birthday, and while some of those things happened, you realized that with privilege comes responsibility. The loan that you signed for meant that you have to make payments. Staying out late meant that you were tired the next day for school or work. The parent thing? That only counted if you weren't still living in their house. You get the picture, you fantasized about all of the great things that would or could happen when you became a legal adult, and then reality set in. The same thing happens during the early years of teaching. (We hope that it takes a few years and not months, because you should linger in this fantasy stage for quite some time.)

It's been a long time since we graduated from college with our teaching degree, but we can both remember how excited we were to join a profession of altruistic people who wanted to make the world a better place by helping our students discover their highest potential. We fantasized about how students would be beyond excited about coming to our classes ready to learn. We would deliver incredible lessons each and everyday and our students would put us up on a pedestal and think we were the greatest thing next to sliced bread. Our administrators would call us rockstars and the list goes on. Truth be told, that may be some teachers' reality, but for us, like so many other educators, that fantasy was fleeting and we were faced with an imperfect system of education. We quickly understood that every classroom was not filled with students who were wide-eyed, bushy tailed, and ready to learn. Many of our students show up with incredible challenges in their lives that affect their readiness to learn. We discovered that, try as we might, some things were out of our control. We had to work harder at finding ways to reach the students who were disenfranchised. Classroom leadership and students' ability to self-regulate caused hiccups in how smoothly instruction happened.

We also got hip really quickly that supplies and materials were not free flowing and you had to make do with less. We were facing a technology boom without the resources and training to utilize technology effectively in the classroom. Administrators were expecting us to learn on our own and deliver engaging lessons using technology without the infrastructure to support it. The copier machine was extremely temperamental and you needed a PhD in copier repair to make the necessary resources for your students.

There were a million and one things to do each day and you never felt like you could get caught up. Taking attendance, writing hall passes, marking papers and grading quizzes and tests, assembling make-up work for students who missed class, meetings, duties, and conferences. The list could go on, but you get the picture. We quickly discovered that we weren't working in Disneyland. It quickly became all about survival.

SURVIVAL STAGE

Talk to any working parent of multiple children and they will regale you with stories of sleepless nights, childcare issues, family members illnesses, paperwork, sports/activities, homework, domestic responsibilities, civic duties, and throw in a few crises here and there and you will see someone in survival mode. You know the look, they always seem like there are too many things to do with not enough time to do them. They may be exhausted with eyes glazed over, and all they can talk about is sleep. Fun is elusive and there is no such thing as time to chill. They worry about every detail and feel like they aren't quite doing anything as well as they would like. They are stretched too thinly.

It's not really all that different for teachers. You are faced with an average of 1500 decisions each day. That's mind blowing! Add to that, lesson planning, classroom management, duties, extra-curricular activities, observations, committees and meetings, technology, new procedures and failed lessons - the list continues. You are just surviving day to day. If you are a fairly new teacher, plan on this season lasting a couple of years. We know, that sounds awful, but be patient with yourself. During this stage, a lot of learning happens and without it you may never become the incredible educator that we know you will be. To move past this stage and get to the mastery level, balance is key. Balancing the many hats that you wear, and the responsibilities that you have as an educator is paramount. In chapter 3 we'll share some insight about self-care.

MASTERY STAGE

"Effective teachers affect lives," says Harry Wong. We all know that there are some very nice teachers out there who will do anything for kids, but truth be told, they are not cutting the mustard when it comes to ensuring that students are learning in an environment that is safe. Being kind and loving to your students will certainly attract many fans, but if the students aren't learning, well, then you aren't doing the job that you are contracted for. School is a learning institution. It's where young minds are shaped and character is built. Educating students is so much more than teaching curriculum, but make no mistake about it, curriculum is an essential part of educating our students. It's your job to ensure that your students are learning and growing in the subject areas that you are teaching, however it happens. Master teachers recognize that. They understand that they need to be an effective teacher so that students can be effective learners.

It's true that as a teacher you may feel like you live in a silo because when you close your classroom door, you have great autonomy. You could spend every day talking about things somewhat loosely related to the subject that you teach and most of the time, it could go unnoticed. The proof, of course, would be in the test scores of your students and their mastery of skills needed to be successful in the following year. Over my years in education, I have had the pleasure of working together with incredible educators who ensured that their students achieved and mastered the skills needed to move on and developed great relationships with

24

their students. I have also had the challenge of remediating students whose teacher did not deliver in terms of instruction, but the students loved their class because they didn't have to work that hard. Often, these teachers had developed great relationships with their students, but they missed on ensuring the mastery of skills. That's a big miss for both the students and the colleagues of that teacher. People will take notice. Year after year, students will move on and the other teachers that inherit the students will notice a trend with students and certain educators. Administrators will take notice. They can tell who the effective and ineffective teachers are. A big part of being considered a master teacher is that you walk a fine line of building relationships with students and understanding their limitations, while holding them accountable for their academic performance and requiring them to reach their best potential.

IMPACT STAGE

We don't need to tell you, you know who some of the top influencers in our world are. They are making an impact whether it be positive or negative. You don't need to look any further than your social media feed to be in the know of the movers and shakers. Who would have ever thought that you could become rich by being a YouTube star, but you can! These creators are making an impact on the world.

It's the same in the teaching world. The most positive impactful teachers are what we consider the superstars. They make a difference in their students' lives. They make connections and build relationships with their students, colleagues, and school community, but they go one step further. They develop engaging lessons and create rigorous learning experiences for their students. They understand how students learn and ensure that they reach all of their students. Teaching is an everyday joy for them, and it shows! Everything they do is done with intentionality. It makes an impact!

Getting to this stage in teaching is a milestone. It says that you were able to remain optimistic and dedicated to the profession that you love. It shows tremendous vulnerability and growth by constantly being reflective and wanting to improve in your craft by becoming or remaining a life-long learner. Sometimes it takes swallowing your pride and giving up a little bit of control with your students, colleagues, and administrators and putting the best interest of your students over your own ego. It will require stepping outside of the proverbial comfort zone and challenging things that are wrong with the system. It will call you to take a stand for what is right, even when it's uncomfortable or unpopular. To make a positive impact in the profession and with your students, you will need to unleash the superstar that is dying to step forward.

When I think of Michele Hill a ton of descriptors run through my head: mentor, life-long educator, caring, organized, thorough, mother, tough-as-nails, leader, trusted colleague, master teacher, friend, motivator, go-to person, passionate, energetic, relevant, forward thinker, and heart of gold. I have had the privilege of working with Michele for many years - to observe her class is a thing of beauty. Her lessons are interactive, out-of-the-box, and extremely relevant. The manner in which she interacts with her students is very interesting. She begins each year the same by hammering home her fundamental 'tough love' beliefs of how her class will be run. After about 3 weeks, they are eating out of her hand. The most interesting part of this process is, once she hooks them, they're hooked for life. The number of former students who come back to visit Michele is mind blowing. Recently, a student came to me in a crisis; as I sat with this student in tears in my office, I realized I needed a different approach, I needed someone who could help ease this student's fears and anxiety. I called Michele; she was in my office in minutes. She immediately put the young lady at ease. I sat back and watched her go to work. Over the next 30 minutes, they shared similar life experiences. Before long, the young lady's stress and fears subsided. The two of them walked out of my office with their arms around each other. This student now has a friend, mentor, and life-coach forever! - Principal, Paul B.

You can move in and out of these stages of teaching throughout your career. You may have reached the mastery level and are feeling pretty darn good about it, and BANG, a life altering event happens, or a shift in your professional role causes you to slide back to stages that you surely moved past. Throw in the birth of a child or two, a pandemic, a marriage, divorce or a health issue into the mix, and you might very well enter survival mode all over again. You may move into a new role as a supervisor or coach, or be asked to teach something totally new and you might find yourself in the fantasy stage once again. When this happens, you may have the roadmap back up or you may not. These setbacks may require that you lean into change, take stock of what you need to do to get back to the stage where you are on solid foundation as a teacher and make a huge impact on the lives of your students. If you did it before, you can do it again. Embrace the challenge and call in support to help you navigate your way through.

Never, ever sell yourself short. Whatever stage that you find yourself in, pause, reflect, ask for help or discover some new strategies and/or resources and chart your course. You will surely discover the pathway into moving forward and leaving a lasting imprint and impact. That will be your legacy.

POINTS TO PONDER

- Currently, where would you place yourself according to the stages of teaching described above? How long have you been there?
- What things do you need to do to move onto the next level?
- How do you ensure that your students are mastering the concepts of your curriculum?
- What is one thing that you can commit to consistently doing that will leave a lasting imprint on your students?
- Are you where you want to be?

CHAPTER THREE

SELF-CARE

"Success at work does not make up for failure at home."
Stephen R. Covey

As you are juggling all aspects of your life, it is important to maintain balance in your professional life as well as your personal life. This includes a healthy you and healthy students in body, mind, heart, and spirit. When you model balance and teach to the whole child, your students understand that you care.

There is a Latin phrase and a Jesuit concept, *Cura Personalis*, that translates to "care for the entire person." *Cura Personalis* was introduced to me for the first time by my oldest daughter, Franki Maria. She attended Saint Joseph's University in Philadelphia, a Jesuit, Catholic school. Her assignment for the university newspaper was to find and interview someone from SJU that witnessed the Pope's visits to Philadelphia in 1978 and in 2015. She discovered the oldest Jesuit priest on campus, Father James W. Moore. During the interview, he proudly told Franki Maria, "If you write anything about me, please write about my commitment to *Cura Personalis*." He was committed to the whole student. He was not focused partially on a domain or a test score or a moment in the academic career of a young adult. Fr. Moore cared about growth in all areas of a person that could eliminate barriers to success and allow people to examine their full potential. He went above and beyond the curriculum because it made sense. That is what all great educators do.

Becoming healthier and staying balanced is a lifestyle. When you are balanced, your potential is within your grasp. Your path leads you to your EPIC: Where your Exceptional talents meet your Passion guided by your Intelligence and Character. Therein lies your EPIC.

As you start organizing your life, begin with goals. In the broadest form of a statement, anytime you want to do something, you should do it, accomplish it. You will have many failures in addition to your many successes. Remarkable things can be achieved when you eliminate common barriers of insignificance, time management, and lack of commitment. Look in the mirror to see not only who you are but who you can become.

That's when the tipping point occurs. Believe in yourself. Keep self-communicating. Self-communication becomes a habit. Self-communication happens when you repeatedly tell yourself what you can accomplish. Make it a part of your routine.

If you have a long-term goal, self-communication must be a continual part of your plan to achieve your goal. Positive self-talk is a component of self-worth. Instead of, "I can't, I can't, I can't," make it, "I can, I can, I can." This will turn into "we can, we can, we can."

BEYOND YOUR COMFORT ZONE IS WHERE YOU BEGIN TO SEE YOUR POTENTIAL

Many times, we ask our students to step outside of their comfort zones to learn new concepts. As educators we must be able to step out of our comfort zones too. When we do, we expand it.

Even when you become a true master of your profession as a teacher, your students will not remember every part of the curriculum you taught. They will however, remember how you made them feel. Students know, through relationship building, if they felt safe, challenged to be creative, and if they "liked" school. Every student will also know if they felt like a test score. Although academic success is important, it cannot be the only component for measurement.

Some of the whole child strategies are simple and others will take broader school planning. For example, there is an overall safety and security plan but you can still greet students at your door and in the hallway to allow them to feel safe. Other safety strategies crossover to the social, emotional aspects of planning.

There were many experiences from your childhood that carry forward your ability to have common sense about teaching and learning. You will reflect on your life experiences and how they influenced these qualities. It is important to embed the connections in theory. Let your students know you as their teacher but also as a person. Some of the best connections that you will make with your students will have nothing to do with the content that you are teaching.

Picture your career as a first year teacher if you used a balanced approach as part of your teaching strategies. This would allow students to become themselves. Many students struggle with their ability to fit into every aspect of life as they grow into this world. As you progressed through school, this may have been you.

Many young people never see themselves in certain roles, including leadership. They see leadership and professional careers for people unlike them. Now is the time to change that perception. We must bring new ideas to the educational arena. We need unconventional ideas as we move towards a different world.

Just like most things in your life, even the conventional paths will not look the same in the not so distant future. Creativity is inspired in many ways and easily incorporated into the classroom strategies and learning methods. Appeal to the interests and passions of your students. Model careers and bring in successful people where the students shift perception to see leadership in all people. Careers with and without college training are equally important.

F At every part of my educational journey there have been bumps and bruises. There will be diversions in your path as well. Sometimes, personal and professional development will be provided, while other times it will be in front of you to seize or create the opportunity. My first full-time teaching position was created because I had a computer programming class at the University of San Francisco. Unfortunately, at the time there was no research on the benefits of technology integration. Digital tools were not yet part of a teacher's repertoire. I observed the students and discovered early on that it was just one of many tools that would contribute to the differentiation of teaching and learning. The trial and error created many failures and success stories. The review of the literature along with my own creative risks contributed to student success. It became evident that some students gravitated towards this new adventure in technology and some did not. One student, Gary, was always out of his chair and around the room. When the new IBM PCs entered the room, he was quick to learn the curriculum and turnkey the knowledge to his classmates. Never be afraid to allow the students to facilitate.

Staying grounded and committed eventually turned into a masters degree and a direction of administration. One cliché has always remained true: "Once a teacher, always a teacher."

I always went where I thought I could be the biggest "difference maker."

Technology infrastructure and digital opportunities change almost every day. Do not become infatuated with fads but depend on the master teachers and your PLNs to guide you. Collaboration and learning from each other will always balance strengths and weaknesses.

As mentioned earlier, balance is an important factor between your personal and professional lives. In your school, one of your goals is student success. As they go beyond their expectations, students become more accountable for their learning. I once worked with a seventh grade teacher that implemented different methods of formative assessment for her students. Each student kept a formative assessment log and wrote down their progress each day for each goal. In this case, a learning objective. You can do the same type of assessment for your own goals. Never be afraid to ask for help. Keep a journal. You will be surprised at how much the journal allows you to reflect. Set your goal, deliver your plan, and chart your progress. Change your plan or method of achievement if you are not mastering the goal or objective. Repeat.

Oftentimes balance is elusive. Professional obligations get in the way of making sure that you have enough energy reserve to take care of yourself and your family. Taking time to do things that enliven you and release stress are just as important as being a superstar teacher. They give you the energy boost that you need to "rock it" in the classroom. We need to take care of ourselves so that we can take care of others.

F In order to reinforce *cura personalis*, set goals in all four areas of you: body, mind, heart, spirit. Balance is important. If you spend all of your time on your mind and never exercise the other areas, you will feel it. In the short term, it can work but in the long term, you will never reach your potential. This approach can and should be modeled for your students. This is an example of my balanced goals for the week that I have used:

- **Body**: Exercise five days per week- Monday (8am), Tuesday (8am), Wednesday (8am), Friday (8am), Saturday (9am).
- **Mind**: Read at least twenty minutes per day, write at least twenty minutes per day, research twice per week.
- **Heart**: Promote leadership on social media. Practice magic four days per week. Family time, dinner, programs, activities.
- **Spirit**: Mindfulness every day. Skateboard or run at least once per week. Wake up each day with love and gratitude. Make leadership and inspirational videos.

Your goals may be different and change from week to week. That is not uncommon. Examine your accomplishments and adjust your plan. Long-term goals will take more planning. Your short-term goals will take planning, too. For example, schedule a time for certain activities. Some decisions have already been made - the time you need to work, the time of certain activities and events like classes and games. These are external forces. Then you can plan your choices. These are activities and events that you can control, like exercise and rest. You can also control your attitude and your ability to achieve most goals. The time in a day is finite, however, it is also renewed every 24 hours.

As you take care of yourself in a more methodical way, you start to see yourself differently. You pull away from seeing leadership as only a title. Self-care becomes a step towards a realization that you are empowered. Your leadership ability will start to emerge. Likewise, when your students begin to see themselves differently, they will define leadership in a different way.

Conversations and perception have convinced us over the years that many teachers do not see themselves as leaders unless they have a title. Our perception is that you are a leader as soon as you cross the threshold of your school building. Your perception of leadership should never be only connected to a title.

Imagine if you understood character and leadership that included self-care at an early age. Then you realize your potential to accomplish anything. Now imagine that every student started character and leadership training. It can be a paradigm shifter.

Whether you have acknowledged it or not, as an educator, you model leadership that includes self-care from all areas of curriculum. You have likely been doing this without recognizing the potential. The perception that leadership can only be positional must be shed and new skin forms with a model of abundance. Students should expect the opportunity to become leaders in your classroom and in the school. Just as many teachers never see themselves as leaders, many young people never see themselves as leaders. They see leadership for only a few. Now is the time to change that perception. We must bring new ideas to the leadership arena. We need unconventional ideas as we move towards a new paradigm. Just like most things in your life, leadership that includes self-care is a process. This would create a shift about the perception of leadership for the top few versus leadership opportunities for everyone. The people at the top of the pyramid come in the least contact with other people. Transformational and servant leadership allow all of us to spend time with people to empower them to take care of themselves and to accept their roles as leaders.

When someone asks me what I do as a profession, I still say that I am a teacher. Even though my new position is more of a leadership position, I identify as a teacher. Truth be told, I developed my leadership skills and attributes as a teacher, and while I have certainly grown in my new role, my core inner leader was created through the opportunities that I was given as a teacher by those who embraced a shared leadership model. To those administrators, I am deeply humbled and aim to pay it forward every day by giving others the opportunity to develop leadership skills.

All teachers are leaders. Teaching and leadership include balance and self-care. When you are healthier, you feel better, your attitude is more positive, and you are more successful. As you see yourself differently, so will your students and colleagues.

POINTS TO PONDER

- What do you need to do each day to make sure that you do not become overwhelmed and stressed?
- What passions do you have outside of your profession?
- What activities or rituals do you do to bring peace back into your daily life?
- What is your personal mission statement? If you do not yet have one, get one.

DOMAIN TWO

BUILDING

CONNECTIONS

WHO'S IN YOUR CIRCLE?

"We are the average of the five people we spend the most time with."
Jim Rohn

A seasoned English teacher would often remind our students "if you lay with dogs, you get fleas." It wasn't the nicest way to remind them that they should be mindful of the company that they kept, but they understood what he meant. Motivational speaker Jim Rohn famously said, "We are the average of the five people we spend the most time with." Take a minute and let that sink in. Who are the five people at your school that you spend the most time with? What qualities do they possess? Are they helping to lift you and the profession of teaching up or down?

This concept of who is in your circle of influence is an important one. It can either make you or break you in terms of your career. To hammer home this point, we do not need to look any further than the political arena that exists in most countries. If your leader goes down, you generally fall with them, and if you are aligned with a winner, you may ride on their coattails. Now, that being said, it may not be as pivotal in your role as an educator, but the people who are in your professional circle definitely have influence over your thoughts, behaviors, and attitude when it comes to your position as a teacher, and other people are watching and taking note.

When I was in college I was required to take a psychology course as a general education class. I asked around about the professors and was encouraged to take a class with a professor who had a reputation for not taking attendance and was an easy grader. The first day of class, I scanned the room and saw some of the "cool" students sitting in the back of the room. I took a seat amongst them and kicked back. I did the required assignments and scored fairly well on the exams, but when grades were posted, I received a D. I was flabbergasted. I couldn't wrap my head around it, so I asked the other students who were seated in the back and they all said that they received the same grade. Boy, did I learn a lesson that day. I realized that I was lumped in with students who were not very ambitious or conscientious. I was judged by the students in my circle. Was it fair? Heck no! The professor was allowing his emotional opinion of me and the group of students to cloud his judgement of my academic performance. I might have been able to appeal the grade, but truthfully, I was so embarrassed by my own behavior of missing class and aligning myself with people who did not have the same work ethic or respect for education that I did, so I took it on the chin. I have never forgotten that lesson. People will judge you by who is in your circle. You have control over that; choose wisely!

When I first started teaching, my administrator took me on a tour of the building and while we were walking, she said. "Let me give you some advice." She proceeded to tell me that it was very important to avoid the negativity of the faculty workstation and lunch room. These two places attract all the faculty at some point in the day. They congregate to make copies, use supplies or gather to eat. Although some of them may be extremely funny and charismatic, be careful about who you buddy up or sit next to; their ideas and behaviors may rub off on you.

I took that advice to heart. Having learned that very powerful lesson while in college, I made it a point to be friendly to everyone, but I chose very carefully who I wanted to work together with on projects, who I sat next to in faculty meetings, and who I allowed to be a part of my inner circle of friends.

Social media is powerful, no doubt! We don't need to tell you that social media can be an amazing resource and platform for connectivity and entertainment, but it can also be a place for negativity and the mob mentality. Let's get the elephant out of the room, your social media accounts are not as private as you believe. The goal of social media is connecting people to others, so it's only reasonable to believe that even if your accounts have great security settings, someone will see your posts and your connections. Who you choose to be friends with, and how you portray yourself through posts and photos on social media can paint a picture of you. What do your social media posts say about you? Have someone objective take a look and give you some feedback.

Be careful of the likes, posts, and comments on social media. It seems innocent enough to like a satirical post of workplace humor, but someone may think that you are unhappy in your profession or you are speaking negatively about your school. Making comments on other people's posts that can be inflammatory or using profane language paints an unprofessional picture of you. Sure, we know, free speech and all, but it's more important to safeguard your public image than it is to be witty.

Not all social media is dangerous. There is an incredible opportunity to build a professional learning network with other teachers across the globe. Connecting with passionate educators outside of your four walls is one of the best ways to stay relevant and continue to grow. The connections that you make with people who are doing innovative things will help to fuel you when you hit the low spots in your career. They can excite you, challenge you, and inspire you to try something new, spread your wings a little (or a lot), and support you in times of need.

We have both benefited from a group of like-minded passionate educators that we affectionately call our PLN (Professional Learning Network). These fine people may or may not live nearby. Most of the time, they reside clearly across the country or even world, but they get us! They support you in your professional, and often, personal endeavors. They show up on social media to be a part of whatever you are working on. It sounds crazy, but they are often who we turn to first to bounce ideas off of, ask for resources, and support and help to elevate the profession.

Our best advice on social media is to create professional accounts to use with the primary goals of connecting with other educators and community members. Lock down your personal accounts so that they are as secure as possible, but know that anything and everything on the internet leaves a digital footprint, so proceed with caution. If you wouldn't want your grandparents to see it, it's probably not prudent to post.

Please don't underestimate the importance of the role of your mentor. Hopefully, your administration paired you up with the best of the best, but if they did not, you can seek out an unofficial mentor who might be willing to help you learn the ropes just the same. Every school is different and every administrator is different. Your official mentor should have received training on how best to assist you to become the best teacher possible and make sure that you are successful. Don't be afraid to be vulnerable and ask for help. That's what they are there for.

In your school, there are many different types of teachers. Some are full of energy and have their hands raised for anything and everything. Truth be told, administrators love these people because they are the worker bees, but some may volunteer to do so many extra things that their teaching suffers. You want to make sure that your primary focus is what's happening in your classroom.

In contrast, another group of teachers are the militant ones who work the exact minutes as outlined by their job description and absolutely not one minute more. We are not telling you that you have to work over contractual hours, but like everything in life, sometimes it's necessary to put in the additional time to ensure that you are prepared for the next day or next week. Do whatever works so that you can feel confident in your preparations and planning to be the best that you can be for your students.

You will want to saddle up next to other passionate teachers who understand the importance of being a professional. They show up each day with a mission to make a positive difference in the lives of their students. They support the school community and extend themselves to the betterment of the school without overextending themselves so that their role as an educator doesn't suffer. They are regarded as true professionals that are admired by the administrators, colleagues, students, and community members. These are the people in your school that you want in your circle. They will help you rise.

What do you spend your time doing during the course of a school week? Write down where you spend your time. Is it where you want to spend your time? Is it with the people you value?

For me, when I became proactive about my life, my life became richer. Author Stephen R. Covey, describes a proactive approach as scheduling your priorities. Your priorities should always include the people you hang out with. People with like-minded thinking and values, find each other and they benefit from those relationships greatly.

Many people find themselves in situations that belittle their worth or the value of what they do. When my eldest daughter declared herself as an education major, several of her teachers from high school responded, "Why do you want to do that?" Not only were they undermining her choice but they depreciated their own self-worth. This leads me to believe that, at some point, they were not happy in their careers as educators. Granted, there is too much bureaucracy, too much teacher bashing, and not enough accolades. We hope this book can change that perception in a positive light.

I can offer many stories of people being steered away from the profession or burnout before tenure. Many correlations are related to lack of support. Conversely, I can offer many stories of people changing careers or shifting gears to become educators and exemplary teachers. Those correlations are related to knowing your why and having people who share it with you.

Before I became a principal, I never realized the impact of climate and culture. As a teacher, my classroom was always a safe place and I valued relationships. Part of the culture breeds support mechanisms but people need to feel they are important and supported in a positive way to take calculated, creative risks. The positive culture mindset will always be a part of my leadership style.

My proactive approach to life and education creates opportunities. If you want something to change, then come up with ideas. Find like-minded people and disrupt the status quo in a positive way. Things do not always have to be done the same way. It's not my way, or your way, but the best way. Those best practices are out there. Keep tapping into your circle.

POINTS TO PONDER

- Who do you spend the most time with during the workday?
- Who do you spend the most time with when not at work?

- Do the people that you spend the most time with exude the qualities that you admire?
- What are your core words? (Words you can live by)

BUILDING RELATIONSHIPS WITH YOUR STUDENTS

"No significant learning occurs without a significant relationship."
Dr. James Comer

F If your students know that you care about them and you love them, they will be committed to their success. They will not want to let you down. Making connections builds capacity in your relationships. There was a student, John, that always came to school early because his mom dropped him off on her way to work. He could be seen on the playground shooting hoops or sitting in the hall on inclement weather days. In the stairwell going up to the eighth-grade classrooms, several students painted a mural of Yoda with one of his famous quotes, "Do or do not, there is no try." For over a year, Yoda's head had an outline but did not have his familiar green coloring. That did not sit well with John. One morning he asked to make Yoda green, like he should be. It was a wonderful idea. The next day Yoda's head was green. How it happened was a mystery but we knew John was the artist. On countless days, John could be seen standing at the bottom of the stairs admiring his masterpiece. He felt important and this simple task connected him to our school forever. He became more engaged and his relationship with us strengthened.

While there are those students who are ignored by others, there are many who take the initiative to connect with classmates in class or during a school event. This can be a cultural perception changer as relationships become long lasting. Common sense tells us to not only connect with the students in our class but with other students as well. It will set the tone. Your schedule may precipitate hall monitoring or outside duty. Initially, it may not be at the top of your list of favorite things to do, but it certainly does give you the opportunity to connect with students who are not in your class. They will appreciate the relationship. It allows them to feel safe and important.

MOver the years, I have forged great relationships with students by going out of my way to greet students as they have passed by my room and engaging them in small talk about some of their accomplishments in their extracurricular activities and sports. It builds rapport and connection. They will know who you are, and you will know them. Make a goal to periodically talk to the students during lunch. Eat with them. In other words, don't let the four walls of your classroom limit you from getting to know the other students in your school. You may just find that you can make the same connections with these students as you do with the one sitting in your classroom—maybe even better!

Although Mrs. Hill was my high school Spanish teacher, the lessons she taught me far exceeded Spanish. She never hesitated to give up her personal time to serve as a mentor and confidant. She was one of the very few support systems I had throughout high school. Her loyalty and support continued into my adulthood, from watching my high school football games to watching me get married. I wouldn't be the man I am today if it weren't for her continued guidance. She is truly considered family. - Josh

FNo school is immune to bad budget years. In order to keep all the instructional staff, some non-instructional employees at our school fell victim to a reduction in force. As principal of the school, my time was probably better spent in other areas. However, I saw the importance, in the short term, to "digging in" and doing "whatever it takes." I rolled up my sleeves, figuratively and literally, and became the lunch room monitor. The students built me a lifeguard stand. It was amazing! Because the chair towered over the cafeteria tables, I could see everyone and everyone could see me. The students started to monitor themselves and clean their own tables. We played music frequently and danced on inclement weather days. Each year, our education foundation held a silent auction. Two of the highest bids were always principal for the day and sitting on the lifeguard stand. Being in the cafeteria allowed me to connect to the students on a different level.

There are a plethora of opportunities to connect. Other years, teachers at our school took the time to help students with simple tasks like shopping for an outfit. Even in affluent districts, students may not have the means to get to a store or buy new clothes for dances. These acts of kind heartedness connect that student to your school forever. Just one person being nice to those who feel disconnected makes an immeasurable difference. As educators, we must try to connect every student to our school. Our theory is that if they aren't connected to school, they may be negatively connected to something else. We have to try to make a difference for that one person that no one else can. You would be surprised at the knowledge you gain from talking to people you never would talk to.

Over our tenure as educators, we can tell you that the kids who need the most love ask for it in the most unloving ways. The students who immediately emerge as behavior problems in your classroom are usually the ones who need positive relationships more than others. They may struggle with issues surrounding trust, authority figures, and insecurity. These issues manifest themselves into acting out in some form or fashion in the classroom and can be challenging to even the most seasoned teacher, unless they find a way to make a connection with the student and develop a positive rapport with them.

Every teacher should make building positive relationships with students a cornerstone of their practice early in the school year. It will set the school year off to a great start. But the challenging students may take some additional effort and time. Often they are testing you to see if you are genuine and you can be trusted. Stay the course, keep building. Day by day, you will make inroads with those students, and soon enough, you will see the budding of a positive relationship and mutual respect for one another. Trust the process.

One year early in my career, I met Chad. I felt as though Chad was determined to make my job as the teacher more difficult. Every day Chad found a new way to disrupt the lesson and cause the entire class to be distracted. As I mentioned, this was very early in my career before I discovered how important it is to develop a positive rapport with students. I tried all of the behavior management techniques that I learned in college, charts, time-outs, conference with the student, phone calls home, but still, Chad persisted to challenge me. I was at a loss, so I used my intuition. I imagined that Chad struggled academically and possibly his act of disrupting the class was a way to cover that he may be very insecure about his abilities. I decided that I was going to love Chad into getting aboard the learning train. So, I did just that. I praised Chad at every opportunity. I supported him with additional resources and assistance, I reaffirmed and guided him when he was off track or struggled. I called home with great news. I had high expectations for him. By the end of the year, the entire class thought that Chad was my favorite student, and secretly, he was. We developed an excellent rapport where Chad was willing to try new things, challenge himself, and ask for help when needed. The funny thing is that the negative behavior disappeared. After that year, I was hooked on developing positive relationships with my students! It worked like a charm.

People like those who are genuine and students are very observant. In order to build positive relationships with your students let them see you for who you really are. Now, of course we are not suggesting showing them the "raw and uncensored" you, but let them see part of your personal life. Show them your sense of humor. Students love to hear about your family, know what you like to do when you are out of school and see your quirky side. You are likely to find that you share some of the same interests or have things in common.

Classroom leadership will either make or break you in the profession, but much of classroom management is about having a solid foundation of good rapport with your students. It's really incredible that having positive relationships with students solves most behavior issues that exist in classrooms today and it all begins with believing in the students and assuming the best of them. It's true that all people have the need to feel a sense of belonging and that begins with acceptance.

If your students know you care, believe that you believe in them, assume that their actions and intentions are good and support them so that they can succeed, you are very likely to encounter few behavioral issues. They will work to keep the relationship a positive one. Now here is the caveat, you must do it with all students, not just the ones that you like. Like we said, students are very observant and if they believe that you only extended those attributes to certain students, you may have more issues on your hands. Be equitable in your approach to developing positive relationships with all of the students, in and out of the classroom.

There are many students that you can engage in conversation with almost every day. Students will jump at every opportunity to be included in your leadership and character training activities. We used the many talents of multiple students for a plethora of positive events that linked our community and other schools.

Fraditions and culture take time to build, and it can become a positive way of life. Not everything appeals to everyone. Keep building anyway. I remember the rough roads. In my first year as principal, I was in the cafeteria and a student jumped on a table. I wasn't sure why but I asked him to get down. He responded with, "You f%&@ing make me?" I started building a relationship with that student immediately. I had to. I simply leaned in and asked if we could talk in the hall. He respected my approach. Even though there were consequences, we started to interact in a positive way because I did not try to embarrass him. Because I was visible and I knew every student, they did not want to disappoint me. Likewise, they knew I would not disappoint them either. My actions and words matched when it came time to be supportive for my students. I held them accountable, but with love and genuine commitment to what was in their best interest.

CONNECT THE DOTS TO YOUR ORGANIZATION AND A LEADERSHIP PICTURE APPEARS

At some point, all great educators struggle with aspects of their job. We may ask ourselves, "Could I have done something differently to reach more students?" "Am I true to who I am and what I believe?" Our words and actions matter when building relationships with our students. Great leaders choose accordingly and understand their consequences. Our true measure of integrity is being able to stand by our words and actions. Speak and act from the heart. Your students will be better for it.

Sometimes instead of focusing on the hundreds of students we reach, we think about those we did not impact positively. If we remain true, we will make a difference and pass on our leadership traits. Believe in yourself, so others will emulate your examples of leadership and love.

Every student needs a positive relationship with an adult in the school building to be successful. The more connected they are to the adult members of the school, the better the odds for success. Make forging relationships a key part of who you are as an educator with all of the students in your building. They will benefit greatly; you will be better for it. It all begins with the relationship!

POINTS TO PONDER

- Who were the most influential teachers that left a lasting impact on who you are today and why?
- How can you ensure that you are building positive relationships with your students without detracting from what you are teaching?
- How do you ensure that you are building relationships with students who are not in your class?
- How important is it to you that you leave a positive imprint on the hearts of your students?

CHAPTER SIX

BUILDING RELATIONSHIPS WITH FAMILIES AND COMMUNITY

"Building relationships is not about transactions, it's about connections."
Michelle Tillis Lederman

Master teachers know that their role doesn't stop at the threshold of their classroom door, it extends well beyond the school campus into extra-curricular activities, community events, and even into the homes of students' families. Creating reciprocal relationships based upon mutual respect and appreciation for a common vision for students is a key component to positive teacher-student relationships and it is a pillar in building strong relationships within the community. When schools, families, and community groups collaborate to support learning, children tend to do better in school, stay in school longer, and like school more. That translates into success for the whole community.

As an educator, you can play a deciding role in making family and community connections that will imprint a culture of trust and partnerships for the students in your schools and the community in which they live. You can be a joiner and connector in numerous ways and in various roles. Let's talk about some ways that you can build important connections to the families of your students and the community at large.

COMMUNITY PARTNERSHIPS

Creating community/business school partnerships is one of the best ways to connect and create an authentic bond with stakeholders. It may require you to go to the people who matter most, and meet them on their own turf. Community walks are a great way to start. Visiting local businesses and community organizations shows that you are extending the proverbial olive branch and can ignite passionate conversations on how to improve both the school and the community and it allows for organic feelings of trust and mutual respect to be built.

When people worship together, something powerful happens. We had a colleague that was very involved in her church and it happened to be the church that many of our students attended. She was able to build important connections with the families of our students while they worshipped together. The church community listened intently when she spoke about school matters with their children. They trusted her and felt that she was acting in the best interest of their children and our students, even when she was telling them something unflattering about their kids. It was a win-win! Make it a point to be visible as often as possible in the community where you plan to work.

Early in my career, I had a superintendent who was a visionary. He declared that our schools would be the mecca of community activity. He knew the importance of creating trust and building connections with the community at large and decided that the best way to achieve this was to invite them in! Nowadays, that is the model for most schools, but back then, it was thinking outside the box. In any case, it works! Hosting community forums, organizational meetings, adult education classes, and extracurricular sports and activities for the whole community is a sure fire way to let people see how great your school is and it is a wonderful bridge between the school and the people who live in the community. If your school doesn't offer opportunities such as these, make the suggestion. Senior Citizen Prom, Trunk or Treat events, egg hunts or scavenger hunts, continuing education classes, social service resource fairs etc. will bring the community to the school and that's a great thing!

HUB OF THE COMMUNITY

How can you create experiences for connecting curriculum through real world applications? Reach out to your local businesses and civic organizations that might allow students to serve in some capacity. The bridge building between students and community is secondary to the relevant experience for the student, but it is equally important. Letting students be part of the community landscape promotes positive relationships with stakeholders.

FBecause we promoted leadership for everyone in our school, servant-leadership became a staple of participation. Each year, we had a service learning platform that went along with our infused character and a common theme. Sometimes the theme was embedded directly into our community. Other times it reached out to our extended community or to a global initiative.

Our community had an outreach organization for cancer patients and their families. One year, we raised enough money for them to establish a local chapter for middle school students. The students were able to visit the facility and participate as facilitators, volunteers, and clients. The biggest component of service is awareness. Our school created publicity for the program that allowed our town to know this place, Gilda's Club, existed.

Another year, we had speakers come in from a rescue mission that was ten miles away. This sparked part of our leadership summit that included service, fundraisers, and volunteering at the mission. The awareness component fueled the realization that we had people in our community or close to our community that needed assistance. Other platforms included hurricane relief, senior citizen connections, green initiatives, and clean water in other countries.

Try having conversations with parents you have never met. It does not matter if the parents are parents of your students. During an evening school event, start the conversation. If you are like most schools, there is at least one event per month that brings in the community. Whether it is a sports contest or a board of education meeting, they happen.

You can build relationships with adults by listening. Sometimes we are too busy talking to listen. We really miss out on a lot of great ideas that will not only make us better leaders but make our schools and organizations better, a lot better.

CREATE A PLACE WHERE EVERYONE WANTS TO BE AND GREAT RESULTS CAN BE ACHIEVED

As part of our commitment to a positive climate and culture, we planned at least one evening event per month where we invited parents and the community. We had movie nights, celebrations of accomplishments, ice cream socials, and events organized by our students.

One fun event was Almost Anything Goes (AAG). It is a series of relay events with students and teachers on ten teams. We invited a team of parents to participate. We packed our gymnasium with ten teams that performed quirky relay races and activities. The culmination is an obstacle course where the team captain gets a shaving cream pie in the face. The purpose is team-building, connections, and fun.

One of the funniest sights is the opening event, The Balloon Break Relay. Balloons are filled with helium and tied to chairs. Each team member runs the length of the floor, grabs a balloon, and sits on it to burst it. Then the team member races back across the floor to tag the next person. It makes for some hysterical times to spend with your colleagues, students, and families to prove we can all laugh at ourselves.

We can reinforce the positive aspects of our relationships. Think about any relationship you have. If you communicate negatively with a colleague, a parent, or a student no matter where you are, your organization will eventually feel it. People will feel the negativity, and they might disconnect by being consumed with adverse feelings. If something is bothering you for good, bad, or indifferent, let your people know.

At any age, people can fall victim to peer pressure. They compromise their personality and their ability to demonstrate their leadership and learning capacity because they care about the persona exemplified by relationships with their acquaintances. You stray away from who you really are.

One night working late in my office and waiting for a board of education meeting to commence, I heard someone come into the main office. I was engrossed in my work so I did not immediately engage him in conversation. I heard this person making phone call after phone call, but I could not hear what he was saying. I went to see who it was. It happened to be one of our teachers. I asked him what he was doing. He said, "I'm making positive phone calls. My goal is ten per month. You won't believe the wonderful reactions I'm getting." Sure, I would! When a new teacher starts in our school, I had them set a goal to positively contact families. Ask them to make a certain number of positive phone calls or any form of contact home per month. It absolutely works. They cannot believe the positive feedback they get when they call the home of a student because they are calling for something positive. It makes quantum leaps in relationship building. Pump out the positives but know that people may still need to vent. Listen and acknowledge. Venting doesn't mean they don't want or need to hear the positives. It means they want to feel heard. We can allow that to happen while making them feel appreciated and understood.

This concept can make an enormous difference in your relationships. One that grows from seeing things the way other people see them. Tunnel vision is a negative perception when you are dealing with people in any type of organization. Where we work, you have to be a parent, grandparent, student, teacher's assistant, teacher, principal, secretary, custodian, maintenance person, United Parcel delivery person, affirmative action officer, crossing guard, bus driver, cafeteria worker, technician, neighbor, community member, politician, police officer, among other roles. You must assume multiple roles wherever you work and play.

PARENT COLLABORATION

It's widely accepted that teacher-parent relationships impact students' learning and well-being, however, it is an untapped resource that is often overlooked. How do you keep the parents of your students in the know? How do you keep them involved in their child's learning?

The old-school way of connecting to families was through a student's report card and parent conferences. Today, that doesn't cut the mustard (old-school phrase, pun intended). Society is different today and so are the families that live in them. Many of our students are in daycare early on. Stay-at-home parents are rare. Parents are carrying an incredible workload of careers and caring for their children and possibly a host of other challenges. We need to meet them where they are and keep lines of communication open both ways.

The evolution of email and social media has increased the ways we can connect with families, but good communication can be phone calls home, text messaging apps, automated calls, newsletters, postcards, and video messages. These set the foundation for a positive relationship with the families of your students. If you don't speak their language, ask for the school to assist with a translator or access an online translator when communicating with your families whose first language you don't share. Speaking of language, be attentive to the language that you are using when addressing family members. Check for titles and familiar relationships to the student. Make sure that you are using expressions that are appropriate and vocabulary that they can understand. Families hang up the phone or close out the email with a warm feeling that they are understood and you are working together as a team to help their children be successful. The most important thing about communication is that it should be often and in various forms.

Inviting parents into the classroom is a dynamic way to strengthen the bond between school and hope. Parents can serve as tutors and resources for instruction. Let's face it, we have some pretty talented parents, grandparents (bonus of cross-generational learning), and guardians who can share their gifts with the students sitting in our classrooms. Tap into the special talents of family members. The families will get a first hand look at the incredible things that you are doing in your classroom and they will spread the word in the community.

I was a Spanish teacher who loved to share, not only the language, but the culture as well. Because I am not hispanic, I could not give first hand experience of traditions. I invited one of the parents of my students to demonstrate making tamales with my class. The parent used a bilingual approach when explaining the process. She talked about the customs and culture of her heritage. The students absolutely loved the experience, and the tamales! Your students will greatly benefit from the expertise of volunteer family and community members in extension activities. Another win-win!

Great teams work together with a shared purpose and common vision. Your students' families are your teammates. They are your partner in ensuring that students can succeed in school and in life. It's important to give them input in decisions affecting their child. Ask questions, and listen. These people know a lot about their children. You will also learn important information about their culture, traditions, passions, and skills.

In the elementary years, the participation of families in their child's education is often much greater than the latter years, but that should not be the case. During adolescence, children are experiencing hormonal changes that can impact decision making. They need adults who are invested in them to assist them and guide them. As teachers, you are in a premier position of influence and can greatly impact a student, however, you are not their parent or guardian. It's very important to keep parents in the loop of important information about their child, particularly non-academic things that may affect them in a negative way. If you feel uncomfortable in discussing such things with the families of your students, seek out a guidance counselor or a member of the administration to assist you.

Over my tenure of teaching, I had the opportunity to teach related students (brothers, sisters, cousins, aunts and uncles, and even fathers and mothers of students). This particular year, I was teaching the youngest child of three of a local family. She was an absolute joy and was in my honors class. I knew her mother quite well after having the older two children, so she felt very comfortable speaking openly to me. I asked about her other two children and she began to tear up. One of her older daughters was experiencing a severe drug issue. My heart sank! I recalled the senior year with her child. I saw that she was hanging around with a very tough crowd and I feared that she was headed down the wrong path, but she was no longer a student in my class. I said nothing. I regret not reaching out to her mother. Her mother's words of, "Why didn't anyone tell me?" haunted me. From that day forward, I decided that I would make sure that parents were informed (someway, even if it wasn't by me) that their child could be in some type of danger. We can change and save lives! When we work together with families to ensure that students are safe, well-adjusted, and are learning, we are building a community of successful people. The story ends happily. This student has been in recovery for many years and has the joy of raising her own children.

It's true, all parents want their children to excel in school, but that is not always the case. Parents/guardians don't know what they don't know. If you haven't communicated issues with them about their child, then they cannot assist you in addressing them.

There are a number of things to consider when seeking support and assistance from the families of your students. Be specific in what you need parents/guardians to do to help their children and provide ways that they can support their child at home. Explain instructional decisions so that families understand the procedures and routines of the school and your classroom, as well as the instructional techniques that you employ in the classroom. It helps them understand what you're doing and why. Our experience has been that family members will ally with you if they believe that you have their child's best interest at heart. If they raise a concern, point them in the right direction for assistance. Let parents know what their child is doing well, what academic skills, social skills or knowledge that they have mastered and any other milestones or achievements. Share the good news through all lines of communication. There is no such thing as too much good news!

SHARE IN THE JOY

Communities are strengthened when people come together in celebration. Almost every community has local celebrations and traditions that you will want to be a part of. Find out what your school community's days of celebration and unique community traditions are and participate in some way.

Show up to local community days and introduce yourself to members of the community. Tell them who you are and what your role in the school is. You will be amazed at the connections that you can make at a craft fair or community day.

Why not level up and join a community committee? Being part of the fabric of an organization creates opportunities for building relationships and impacting the experiences of all members from the community. If you don't reside in that particular community, people will be greatly impressed by your willingness to devote your time, energy, and talents to them.

POINTS TO PONDER

- Where is the place that is considered the central hub of your school community? How can you gain access and/or be a participant in the activities taking place there?
- How can you attract community members to your school and to partner with your school community?
- How can you connect your students to the community to do outreach?

DOMAIN THREE PROMOTING RESPECT AND CITIZENSHIP

EQUITY AND DIVERSITY

"The time is always right to do what is right."
Martin Luther King, Jr.

It wasn't until recently that people could discern the difference between equality and equity. We've been hearing the term equality since the sixties with the Civil Rights Movement and Feminism. We certainly want equality, but equity is the pathway on how we hope to get to equality. Equity is giving people the tools, resources, and opportunities to level the playing field for all. It's about wanting to see everyone succeed.

Ensuring that everyone gets what they need to be successful is certainly different than giving everyone the same things. Everyone's starting point is different. Our students come to us with diverse backgrounds, their availability of resources, their unique cultures, and different family dynamics, so it would only be reasonable for us to assume that if we want our students to reach the same benchmarks for success, we will need to support students differently. Creating a culturally responsive classroom and school environment is paramount for ensuring that all students have an opportunity to succeed. Before we talk about what you can do to create an inclusive and equitable classroom, you will have some work to do. Have you checked yourself? This is internal work and requires us to be introspective and reflective.

Implicit bias is when we have attitudes towards people or associate stereotypes with them without our conscious knowledge. Now, here's the thing, you may not even be aware of your own implicit bias towards groups of people who are different from you. Most of us see ourselves as a good person who accepts everyone based upon their character, but the research shows that our brain is averse to things that are unfamiliar to us and that our implicit biases often predict how we'll behave more accurately than our conscious values. In order for us to create a culture of being responsive to all learners, we must examine our own implicit biases. Your first step is to take an implicit bias test to uncover your own implicit biases. Once you uncover them, you will need to make a concerted effort to recognize when these biases cause an emotional response and retrain your brain on how to shift your actions. I have found myself recognizing situations where I am aware of a heightened emotional response to groups of people that I have an implicit bias about. I immediately stop and take a moment to think about the situation and ask myself a few key questions:

- Why am I uncomfortable or feeling anxious?
- Is my response to the situation or person in alignment with my core values of treating everyone with dignity and respect?
- How can I reduce my own anxiety in this situation?
- What more do I need to know or do to make sure that I am honoring everyone's diversity?
- How can I be more inclusive for all parties?

It will take some time to make the shift, but once you do, your brain will recognize new associations and actions and your relationships with diverse people will improve.

Familiarize yourself with the diversity of people in your school community. Do some digging into your school's demographics and get familiar with the different groups of people in your school. Once you have the demographic information, the important work begins. Check out the important aspects of the diverse cultures of your students and their families. Foster a sense of community and togetherness by celebrating together.

In our school, we had a showcase night that invited members of the community to come see what we do best in our schools. It's a great opportunity to make important community connections and bring people together. Our World Language Department would host a celebration of cultural diversity through food. Families were invited to make a cultural food favorite and share the recipe. You could see the pride in our students and their families! They beamed!

Don't forget to include representatives from the different groups of people in the planning of events. The more opportunities that you create to promote acceptance and recognition of diversity, the more success that you will have with your students and their families. Make sure that you are aware of cultural norms within your school community and your students. Phrases, greetings, and non-verbal communication may be very different with different groups of people. Ensure that you are using modes of communication and actions that all people find acceptable. Stereotypes can influence what we think we know about others. Avoiding prejudices and perpetuating stereotypes in your communication with students and their families is essential. If you have questions, do your research. Learn about cultural practices that are unfamiliar to you. Seek out those in your PLN who have committed themselves to teaching others about equity and diversity. Creating a bond between families and schools can look different for different students. The traditional model of school invited families in. You may have to go out to build the bridge between school and family.

Every educator should be thinking about how to ensure that each and every student feels safe and that they belong in your classroom. The strategies and ideas that promote a culturally responsive classroom and school benefit all students.

It's pretty safe to say that we have all felt like we didn't belong somewhere in our lives. Creating a culture in your classroom where every student feels a strong sense of belonging and is accepted for their uniqueness is paramount over any curriculum and instructional strategies. It's the foundation upon which learning happens. So how do you do it? What do you do that makes every student feel like they can be themselves when they are in your classroom?

It's so important that your students see themselves reflected in your school and in your classroom. Representation matters! The selection of resources, textbooks, and room decor should include a high level of diversity. The dimensions of diversity include, but are not limited to, ancestry, culture, ethnicity, gender, gender identity, language, physical and intellectual ability, race, religion, gender, sexual orientation, and socio-economic status. Your students should feel a sense of belonging in their classroom. They should be a part of creating the classroom. They should have a say in the learning that occurs. They should feel that their voice matters. When we acknowledge, embrace, and value the diverse nature of our classrooms, all students benefit.

Being an inclusive practitioner means that communication and the decision-making process will not discriminate against individuals or treat them unfairly on the basis of differences. Let that sink in. How do you make sure that all of your students have a voice in the classroom? How do you make sure that they all have a seat at the decision-making table? How do you include all students in opportunities for growth and success? How do you promote building relationships amongst all students? How you interact with each student is being witnessed by all of the other students in your classroom. They can tell which teachers don't like which students. Your verbal and non-verbal communication says it all. Students know and they feel it. Are you an inclusive or exclusive practitioner?

The physical design and routines of the classroom can greatly affect the opportunities that students have to build relationships and cultivate a culture of empathy amongst themselves and their peers. Pods or group seating arrangements that are designed intentionally to bring together different types of students helps to make important connections and friendships. The key is to rotate the groups so that students have the opportunity to become acquainted with each other. The rituals that you set forth in the classroom will also yield opportunities for deeper connections and relationships that will promote acceptance and celebration of commonalities and differences.

On the first day of school, most teachers review the classroom rules with students - raise your hands, ask for a lavatory pass, don't talk when others are speaking, and so on. These are an attempt to create group norms for the classroom so that learning can happen and people are respected. There are some norms that do not make it to the list of classroom rules, but are critical to creating a culturally responsive classroom and should be included. Sure, we all promote being respectful, but do we specifically say that there will be no pejorative language being used, or actions that offend someone's race, gender, socio-economic status, religion, and abilities? Probably not, but we should. Setting norms in your classroom needs to be explicit and specific. Together, your class should create a doctrine of group and individual norms that will be honored by everyone with a focus on inclusivity, mutual respect, and honoring one another. What's one group norm that you can change to ensure that all students feel like they are being respected?

Helping students is in our DNA as a teacher. Well, not really, but you know what we mean. It's a core value. We help students with their academics, help them to discover their passions, help them to learn how to compete; the list could go on and on, but do we help them to celebrate their differences?

I'll never forget the day that Leonardo, a high school student, asked the school photographer to *"paint me white"* when taking a picture of him with his friends during spirit week. When I asked Leonardo why he asked that, he responded so quickly, "So I can be like everyone else." I was shocked, and immediately felt sad—not just for Leo, but for us as a society. It was at that moment that I began a journey to understand how it must feel to be different from the dominant group of people, and more importantly, how could I help those students feel as though they belong without giving up the essence of who they are.

The gravitational pull of "fitting in" is very strong, and some may feel that they have to shed or cover up their cultural diversity to others. That's where you come in. Your role as a teacher puts you in an extremely impactful position. Our students need us to reinforce that what makes them different is also what makes them special. We must make sure that we are not asking them to adopt the dominant culture by changing their name in any way, hiding their core beliefs and rituals, playing small in terms of their skills, and sacrificing their morals and values to fit in. Help them to discover who they truly are, to embrace what makes them different, and to walk confidently in their own skin.

Seeing yourself as different can have a profound effect on your success. You may not see who you are or realize who you can become. If people do not see themselves in a certain profession or role because of their race, gender, socio-economic status, etc., they may not pursue a certain career, club, hobby, or area of learning. Likewise, they must view themselves as competent. Give your students opportunities at an early age to see themselves as successful. In all areas of curriculum, we can show examples of different races and genders that have and continue to play a role in all types of careers.

Try differentiating according to passion. Think about how powerful that can be. My whole life as an educator, differentiating instruction according to a student's or an adult's passion should have been common sense. Once I saw it done, it became commonplace. I witnessed the power of passion in colleagues, teenagers, young adolescents, and children. When students are able to facilitate learning to other students about their passion, amazing outcomes happen. They find a new direction because they see themselves differently.

The impact of a teacher is not just felt inside the walls of the classroom. You are part of a bigger community, the educational community. Your role as an inclusive practitioner is not just reserved for your students. You may have heard the saying "I can only control what goes on in my classroom, so that's what I worry about." That type of thinking can perpetuate inequities and injustices for our students if you are sticking your head in the sand about things that may be happening in other places in our school community or society as a whole. It is true that we may be limited in what we can do and say, so we understand that it may not be possible to react or rise up to every situation that screams inequity, but we can do something to shine a light for others to see. You may choose to call in an expert or channel up your concerns, but make no mistake, ignoring issues is not the right thing to do.

Ensuring that our schools are equitable and inclusive for all of our students doesn't just happen in our classroom. It is incumbent upon you that you challenge the inequities and injustices amongst your colleagues, in your school, and in society by speaking up when things are wrong, advocating for diversity, and leading with a mission for equity for all. Does your school have a committee of stakeholders that are dedicated to equity and diversity? If not, how about volunteering to lead one? Students, staff, administrators, and community members should be examining curriculum, evaluating resources for cultural and diversity content, inventorying the needs of students, and allocating or re-allocating funds to ensure that all students have access to the resources that they need to be successful. Holding roundtable conversations on ways to bring to light the most pressing issues facing our diverse groups with possible solutions and finding ways to elevate the messages of tolerance, acceptance, and celebration of all. Get *fired up* about being an advocate for the beautiful mosaic of people in your school community. Remember at the on-set of this book we said, "It all starts with you!"

POINTS TO PONDER

- Think back on your childhood and your family dynamics. What implicit biases were passed on to you?
- After reading this chapter, what group norms can you create to ensure that all students feel a strong sense of belonging and that they feel valued and respected?
- What strategies do you have in place to make strong connections with the families of your students?
- How can you elevate the message of diversity and equity in your school community?

PROCEDURES AND ROUTINES

"You'll never change your life until you change something you do daily."
Sohn Maxwell

Disclaimer: This book is intended to get you *fired up*, and we certainly want to deliver that experience as you read this book. This chapter is dedicated to the importance of routines, procedures, and classroom leadership. It will be the heaviest in the book in terms of practical strategies that will impact you everyday as a teacher. Trust us when we say that classroom leadership styles can either make or break a teacher and how you effectively manage the many issues or challenges faced in a classroom is key for student and teacher success.

As I have evolved as an educator, my opinions of a grading system have changed significantly. This mindset shift has occurred by observing hundreds of teachers, visiting dozens of schools, and collaborating with educators around the world. Because of my many opportunities to observe, I have come to the realization that we are creating inventors, poets, writers, engineers, and teachers. We are also inspiring plumbers, electricians, carpenters, and architects. When the proverbial lightbulb goes on to your teaching delivery, you will know it. Unfortunately, in your state, province, or country, you may be forever judged and tied to your standardized test scores. Disrupting the status quo for positive change is shunned by a lot of schools. I was fortunate to be in places where I was able to be a disruptor. I hope you are, too. Although you may be linked to a grading system in your school or district, you are not bound by your delivery methods. A teaching toolbox has continual growth. I always looked for better ways to teach and learn. We should be in constant search of the best methodologies. What I was able to document was that there was a strong correlation to a positive culture and positive performance. Culture begins in your classroom and carries into the hallways and other areas of your school. From my first year to my second year as principal, discipline referrals were cut in half. They were cut in half again in the third and fourth years. This came from everyone creating a place where we wanted to be. We developed a positive climate and culture through leadership opportunities for everyone. A big part of our leadership for the students was an emphasis on character and kindness. We highlighted the positives and held school wide events that celebrated our success.

There will always be consequences for negative behavior but the positive outcomes should always be celebrated on a much larger level. If your school experiences a catastrophic event or your standardized test scores are subpar, people will make it newsworthy. Shift the paradigm by making the positives newsworthy.

Students need structure. We all do. Most people have the idea that they would love to have no alarm clock to wake up to, no schedule for the day, no lists of things to do, and certainly no negative consequences for undesirable behavior. We get it! It sounds dreamy, but it's not realistic unless you are retired and living on a remote island. Most people need structure to be successful. They need a routine to follow and procedures that make the path easier. For our students, having a routine and following procedures is optimal for success. It is also critical for the day to day operations of a school.

Imagine the cafeteria filled with hundreds of students clamoring in to get lunch. Devoid of procedures and routines, this could be chaos. The need for structure in school is paramount. When visiting other schools, you can immediately tell which ones have a predictable routine and procedures in place that promote safety and protect the well being of students and staff, and which ones are struggling with set norms and procedures that create healthy boundaries. It's abundantly clear that great schools have successfully established routines and procedures, and it's abundantly clear to administrators when they walk into a classroom where routines have been established and procedures are being followed.

Always be cognizant of your teaching and learning goals with a proactive approach. Teach as though every parent and administrator were in your class along with your students. There should not be a special lesson when you think a supervisor might walk in. Everyone should know your intended outcome.

Lessons are designed for the students, not the administrators. Calculated, creative risks can be taken when teachers are empowered to take them. You should feel comfortable to use new techniques because personal and professional development is encouraged and should be provided.

As a building principal, one of my daily goals was to visit every classroom every day. That gave me knowledge of some phenomenally great teaching. These same visits could also raise a red flag. I was thrilled to throw myself into the mix. Your administrators may observe you only formally, or they may be in your room frequently. Great administrators separate themselves by visibility. They do not just show up when something is wrong or to fulfill an obligation.

Set the tone as your students enter the classroom. Some teachers have their students lineup before they enter. Other teachers give high fives or a verbal greeting. The best teachers always meet their students in some form. It builds relationships and it promotes kindness. Think about that. Do you want to be greeted with politeness when you enter a room? The answer is yes! Even with remote learning, teachers become creative in relationship building and greeting students.

It does not take an entire class period for an outsider to determine the effectiveness of a lesson. The students should be engaged in learning that is meaningful and exciting. Granted, every lesson may not be thrilling but there are multiple ways to stimulate a classroom. Visible transitions, cooperative learning, diversified formative assessment, higher level questioning, among other teaching methods are obvious. Students are aware of expected outcomes and class requirements. They are posted, recited, and accomplished.

Seating arrangements are sometimes determined by the size of the room and available furniture. It is up to you as a teacher to arrange and rearrange the desks or chairs differently to create effectiveness. Innovative teaching takes hard work and commitment. Sometimes it is trial and error when you use new ideas and strategies. Never be afraid to ask the opinion of your students.

Great educators know that all students learn differently. Even within the clusters of learners, differentiating is necessary. What happens when we don't differentiate for our students? We are not setting up students for success. Teachers would not do that intentionally, but that may indeed be the by-product of failing to differentiate for our learners.

When I was a teacher, I had a routine that fit the classes I was teaching. Always be fair and consistent. Sometimes the same curriculum needed to be differentiated not only for a multitude of students but also for the time of day that changed those same personalities. I always greeted my students. They expected it, and I never let them down. I allowed the students to facilitate when it was appropriate. They knew the rules, the consequences, and the rewards. With the rewards came more responsibility. They enjoyed my class, and they knew I loved them and appreciated them because I told them. I modeled positive behavior. As part of a normal observation as a principal, I visited a social studies class. The lesson was a component of the American Civil War unit. The teacher was a master at integrating primary source documents, media clips, text excerpts, and assessment to completely engage his students. The assessment was project based by choice. A student went to the front of class to make a presentation about baseball during the Civil War era. Baseball was his passion. His presentation was outstanding. The student became another class facilitator for the unit. The other students asked questions until the period ended. From that day forward, the student was a different person. He was always smiling and eager to talk to his teachers and peers. They were anxious to interact with him, too. He became a database for a game many in the class liked, baseball. He had a new persona that included being connected. He saw himself as a different person.

One of my students took longer than most to process new information. When I spoke to him, there was often a pause, and you could sense that he was really thinking hard about what I was saying. I knew that this student needed additional time to process information and oftentimes, a different instructional strategy. I built in additional time for all activities related to this student. Sometimes it required him to come back for extra help or to complete the activity, but it was a necessary accommodation to ensure that he was successful in mastering the information and skills. I also incorporated a variety of instructional strategies that hit different modalities for learning. Unfortunately, some of this student's other teachers didn't embrace differentiation and the student was failing their classes. They timed all of their activities and did not give additional time and they had one way of instructing a concept. Their view was that you either got it or you didn't. He didn't. His failure was as much his teachers' failures. Be the teacher that ensures that every student can learn in your class. Get to know your students' learning styles and differentiate accordingly. Differentiation is equity at it's finest. You are ensuring that all students have what they need to be successful in the learning environment. When my students walked in on the first day of school, I let them sit where they wanted to and spent time building relationships. By the end of the first week, I could tell who should be together and who shouldn't. I would then develop the seating chart. As you feel more comfortable in your ability to lead your students, you can change your seating assignments to a more flexible design. Flexible seating designs can be very trendy, and certainly progressive for student collaboration, but they can also be a nightmare for new teachers trying to establish classroom procedures. Give yourself adequate time to develop a strong rapport with students and clear expectations of the classroom routines.

When people know what to expect, they are less anxious and more likely to be amicable to the rules and regulations of the institution. The classroom is certainly no different. The need for established routines in a classroom is so important that they have made it a key component of teacher evaluations. When your students walk through the door of your classroom, they should know what to do immediately, not left wondering what's happening and giving them an opportunity to negatively impact the learning environment. That's not to say that students should not have input into creating the classroom culture, they certainly should, but the overall onus of ensuring that your classroom is a safe environment for learning is on you. Developing routines and procedures that maximize the likelihood of success is also up to you.

At the beginning of the school year, make it clear and spell out the rules, consequences, and even procedures making the invisible visible in your classroom and throughout the school. Relay to students that the rules and procedures are there to keep them safe and protect everyone's right to learn.

Teach and reinforce the expectations of the classroom so students always know what comes next. This is not to say that you cannot be flexible or change things up, but students should be able to predict a rhythm of how your classroom functions. Routines take time, but they are worth the investment.

Start by greeting students at the door and directing them to their "do now" or "bell ringer" activity to get them situated and prepared to work. Develop transitions from one activity to another that help reinforce the routines and procedures set forth in your class. Once students have become accustomed to the routine, they crave it and it becomes automated.

Set procedures for everyday activities such as collecting papers or distributing books and materials, issuing lavatory or hall passes. Routine events should be predictable. There are many things that can distract students or hijack time in your classroom, so having procedures in place will help to keep things running smoothly.

STUDENT CONDUCT

"We will love your kids to death, but we will hold them accountable!" Those words were spoken every year by a principal we knew at the new student orientation. He wanted families to know that *because* we love their children, we would hold them accountable for their actions—and we did!

Kids are observant. There are thirty of them watching one of you. They are fixated on what you do, what you say, and your mannerisms. Don't believe us, ask them to imitate any one of their teachers and their impressions are spot on. They are watching your interactions with students and paying attention to how you reinforce the procedures in your classroom, and if you are holding everyone accountable by the same measure. They will call you to the carpet if you have favorites or levy unjust consequences for some over others.

When I first started teaching, I had an administrator who gave me some sage advice. She said, don't let the students see you sweat. Not literally, but don't let the students see that you are anxious, intimidated or highly emotional. While some might argue with this advice, it served me well at the beginning of my career as a teacher. Kids aren't likely to follow someone if they think that you don't know what you are doing—and they will challenge you if they think they can.

Most people can look back on their school experience and recollect different teachers and styles of classroom management they had. You were likely to have some teachers who were highly emotional and reacted to student misbehavior with outward signs of frustration like yelling, eye-rolling, heavy sighs—you get the picture. What these teachers didn't realize is that they were creating tension in the classroom and making students feel unnerved. When you let students get under your skin, you can create a sense of distrust and resentment, causing students to challenge your authority and test you when the opportunity arises. Each time you allow your emotions to dictate your reactions, you give away your power of controlling the learning environment. You send very strong signals that your peace is dependent on how the students in your class behave; you shift control over to the students. And once this happens, it's a constant uphill battle. When you react negatively to students' behaviors, you shift the accountability from their behavior to you, where they can direct anger at you.

Reacting emotionally to a student's behavior is a sure-fire way to cloud your judgement and say or do things that you are likely to regret. You run the risk of alienating your students.

Your goal for classroom management is to create a safe learning environment for all students. They should know what is expected of them and know exactly what will happen if they don't meet those expectations.

You may be wondering, how do I remain calm and in control when faced with student conduct issues? We have some tried and true strategies to ensure that your classroom is a place for learning.

NON VERBAL EXPRESSIONS OR GESTURES

You know it as the "teacher look" accompanied by teacher proximity. You may actually have to practice your "teacher look" in the mirror and perfect the face that says that you mean business, while being calm and in control. Giving students the "look" is highly effective at curtailing behavior issues. The great benefit of this strategy is that there is no loss of instructional time and the relationship between teacher and students remains friendly and respectful.

Body language and proximity are great ways to redirect students who are off-task or misbehaving. Standing near students generally keeps them working and behaving appropriately. Throw in a few gestures that indicate what you want them to be doing and voila, they get back on track. Contrary to popular belief, most students want to be seen as "good kids" and want positive affirmations.

VERBAL CORRECTION OR WARNING

The look, gestures, and moving close to them didn't work? You may have to give a warning or a verbal correction. The goal is always to give a correction in private or as quietly as possible. When you give a verbal correction, remove the emotion, state the directive and keep moving with the lesson. You might try a strategy of not calling them out individually. For example, you might say "I need 3 people to follow me, or get back in the game." This strategy helps them to self-correct. Make sure to follow up with something positive so that the students recognize that it is the behavior that is unwanted, not them.

CONSEQUENCE

People often refer to consequences as discipline, but not all consequences are negative. The end goal of levying consequences for unwanted behavior is to change the behavior and get them to think about their actions. When it comes to holding students accountable for their actions, just like a parent, you need to mean what you say and do what you say. Following through is just as important as having the expectations in the first place. Idle threats of hanging your child up by their toes are not taken seriously (thank goodness), but they send a message that you might be full of hot air and not serious about holding them accountable.

Consider the following:
• Heart to heart talks with students
• Changing seats
• Time outs in another space in the room or another classroom
• Written or verbal apologies
• Research the cost of things damaged or who is affected
• Reflection sheet (why they did what they did, what could they do differently and how they feel about the situation.)

Whatever the consequence you decide on, make sure that it matches the infraction in severity, upholds your commitment to treat students with respect, and that you document all of the details to share with parents, counselors and administrators. Consistency for consequences is key. If you are consistent, you will likely have less opportunities to enforce the rule. If you are inconsistent, you will likely have to escalate your consequences to change the behavior.

PARENT CONTACT

A word to the wise, the first time that you contact a parent should never be about their child's negative behavior. Get the school year off to a great start and contact parents to let them know how excited you are to have their child in your class. Tell them a little bit about yourself and what the expectations are for their child. They are more likely to be supportive if you started off on a positive note. If you see a pattern emerging with a student, make another connection with the parent and ask, "What do I need to know to ensure that your child is successful in my class?" This question intimates that you are interested in assisting their child in any way that you can—and you are! It is also likely to give you useful information that will help you build a more positive relationship with both the student and their family.

No one likes to make the dreaded parent contact about undesirable behavior of a student, but sometimes it is necessary. Phrase your communication in as positive a manner as possible so the parent knows you genuinely like the child but you are holding them responsible for the unwanted behavior. Allow the parent to speak and be heard. This is very important. Give the facts of the incident and the consequences and ask the parent to support you. Nine times out of ten, parents are on your side and will work with you to resolve the issue with the student.

REFERRAL TO THE OFFICE

This is absolutely your last option, but it may be a necessary one. Administrators will tell you that you should make every attempt to handle issues in your classroom. You might be thinking that that's their job—and it is, however they know that once they intervene, they are controlling the situation, not you. Some behaviors are completely out of your lane to deal with. They are non-negotiable infractions that require an immediate referral. Others may just be that you have tried everything to curb the unwanted behavior. In this case, it's okay to ask for help. Work together with your administrator on strategies to change the behavior or assist the student with skills for better decision making.

GRADES AND ASSESSMENTS

What is the purpose of grades and assessment? The real answer is to have proof of learning. Some schools are very progressive and have moved into standards-based proficiency grading systems, but the majority of schools are still using grades and assessments as the gauge of whether students are learning—and if teachers are effective.

We are challenging you to create assessments that demonstrate mastery, not a "gotcha". We all have had the experience of that teacher who created a test with information that they never taught or designed the test so hard that no one got 100. It was like a badge of honor for them. But why? Your assessment should be created as a way that students can demonstrate mastery of the skills taught. Period. If all students demonstrate mastery at 100%, you have done an awesome job of teaching the required skills. Kudos to you! Just make sure that your assessments are in line with the standards of required benchmarks.

M I worked with a high school teacher who had a policy of never giving less than a 50 for the first two report cards, even when students were failing with a lower grade. Being a novice teacher, I was set on making sure that I held students accountable for their behavior and their work ethic. This policy was in direct opposition to my accountability rule. It irked me that a student who hadn't worked hard enough would be given something that they didn't earn. It wasn't until a few years later that I discovered the genius of his policy. It keeps kids in the grade game, meaning they can recover from a poor start. We are all familiar with grades and averages. Students need a certain numerical or letter grade average to pass for the year. If they are numerically out of the game right out of the gate, they stop trying and can become behavior problems. If they have a 50, they can recover. They will need to really work hard, but it's possible. This may be more applicable to middle and high school, but it is worth mentioning that in the elementary grades, assigning failing grades will likely cause self-esteem issues that carry over into the middle and high school years.

A few caveats about grades:
- Please do not ever use grades as punishment. If grades are intended to show proficiency of skills, behavior does not enter the rubric.
- Deadlines are great, and necessary, but do not deduct so many points on late work that students fail to turn in assignments altogether. Students will never know how capable they are, if they reached their learning target, or progressed toward learning if they don't complete the assignment. Lateness is unrelated to the desired skills.
- Do overs are not cheating. You can allow students to redo an assessment and ensure the fidelity of the assessment by creating an alternate assessment tool to demonstrate mastery. It's a win-win!
- Grades should reflect their proficiency, not the average of their previous grades. You can adjust their final grade to reflect their mastery of the skills and/or information.
- Grade assignments on accuracy not completion. This one change will ensure that students are completing the assignments and developing desired skills. If you grade assignments on competitions, they will likely write in any answer, copy from one another or not pay attention to detail.

IMPAIRED STUDENTS

M I don't remember if college education classes ever touched on the topic of what to do if you believe that one of your students may be under the influence of drugs or alcohol, but if yours did, kudos to the professor bold enough to touch on the taboo topic. We all hope that this will never be something that we have to do in our classrooms but sometimes the need arises.

As a high school teacher, I have had many situations where I needed to make the call. So, what do you do? Each district is different in terms of who to contact first. Your school administrators should share this information with you. If they don't, ask. It is important that you do not sweep it under the rug. You could literally save a student's life.

I was always very observant of my students' behaviors. I could tell when they were having an off day. I also grew up in the 70s so I knew that drugs were a thing to be cautious of and could recognize the signs of drug use. Toward the latter part of my teaching career, I started to hear about and see the use of prescription pills permeate the high school. We had students in full blown addiction to opioid drugs. Parents and staff were not prepared in any shape or form to deal with the epidemic, but we came together to share important information on the dangers of drugs in our community. Our school district tackled this issue head on, but it required staff members to be aware and understand that you are not getting students into trouble, you are possibly saving lives or steering them away from danger.

Over the years, I have had many students walk through the door with baggage that affects them in many ways. High school is a pivotal time for all students. It's the first time they get so much freedom to make choices about who they spend their time with and what they do with that time. Unfortunately, this is the time that many experiment with drugs. A very shy and young student arrived with a pleasant attitude, but I could sense that his story was not being told. Soon after the beginning of the year, he was falling asleep often in my class and was generally disengaged. He was amenable, but not attentive. One day, I noticed that he was showing signs of being under the influence. It was the last period of the day, and on a Friday no less, but I had to refer him for a drug screening. That meant that an administrator had to accompany him to the hospital for a test. He came back with positive results for marijuana. I wish I could tell you that this was his wake up call, but it wasn't. Over the next three years, this student was scheduled for my class again and again (because he failed it and needed the credits.) I told him, "Please know that if you come to my class impaired, I will refer you for help because I love you and care about you." He struggled for years with addiction. Recently, he came back to say thank you and to tell me that he was recovering. He knew that my intentions were to help him, not punish him. Not only is it your professional duty to refer impaired students to administration, it is an act of love for your students. You can change the trajectory of their lives.

A successful classroom requires finesse. It is a combination of great instruction, positive relationships, set boundaries with consistent consequences, and being firm and fair with all of the students in your classroom. Routines, procedures, and engaging lessons, with positive reinforcement, are essential to creating a space for learning. How you lead your class is paramount. Take the time to build teachership skills in your classroom—it will pay off for years to come!

POINTS TO PONDER

- What are your established routines and procedures?
- After reading this chapter, where do you see areas that you need to work?

- How much time in each class is spent on managing behaviors?
- What classifies a lesson as engaging?

DOMAIN FOUR
MAKING AN
IMPACT

CHAPTER NINE

BE A CHEERLEADER

"Let's cheer each other on and watch each other grow!"
Stephanie May Wilson

You can't spell cheerleader without the word leader. By this point in the book, you have learned so much about becoming a teacher leader and you should recognize that master teachers wear many hats. We are adding the hat, or title, of cheerleader to the role of any passionate educator who aims to make a difference. Why? Because showing up and showing out in support of your school and students demonstrates your commitment to your profession for everyone watching. In a previous chapter, we talked about the importance of showing up for community and school events, but we are going to take it to another level. Cheerleaders, are you ready?

Both of our daughters were competition cheerleaders. We have spent countless hours in gymnasiums waiting for our daughters' teams to compete. We would not only show up, we had signs, we cheered and yelled words of affirmation, along with occasional fog horns and whistle blowing. It was pretty obvious that we wanted them to know that we were there to support them. We wouldn't have missed it for the world and they were counting on us to cheer them on—and so are your students, colleagues, and the community. They want to feel your support and pride. They want to know that they are important enough to not only show up, but carry signs (literally and figuratively) of support and cheer in any way that you can. It matters!

In the classroom, having a positive energy has shown to yield great results in building a relationship between teacher and student. Positive reinforcement is, or should be, the main approach to getting students to follow the group norms established for learning. So, being a cheerleader for your students while in your classroom shouldn't seem like too far of a stretch. Make sure that you know each student by name early on. It shows them that they are important to you.

I used to make it a challenge during the first few weeks of school to know every student by name by a certain date. If I missed one, I made the whole group brownies. Sure, they were cheering me on to miss, but they were equally as excited that I knew each and every one of them by name. It was a great way to start off the school year.

If you aren't familiar with the 5 Languages of Love, it's a great and easy read. One of the love languages is words of affirmation. In your classroom, make a concerted effort to affirm your students on high quality assignments, great work effort, following established procedures and rules, character education traits and so on. Maximize the positive and minimize the negative. Sounds simple enough, but this has not always been the go-to method for teaching. Punishment and drawing attention to the negative has been too popular and often taught as a way to control students. If that has been your experience, take a few moments to re-read chapter 8 on creating procedures and routines that work.

Words matter. Don't believe us? Look at the following phrases and see the subtle difference in the word choice, but how the impact is quite profound:

I am confident that you are able to master this. vs. *I hope that you will be able to do this.*

I knew that you were capable of overcoming a very big challenge, but you exceeded my expectations. vs. *I wasn't sure that you would be able to rise to the challenge, but you did.*

You always behave in a way that makes me proud. I know that you will do that today. vs. *I expect you to be on your best behavior.*

The language that you use sends a message to your students and their families. It should say, "I believe in you, I am proud of you, I care about you." It should infer that they are accepted, valued, and supported. Choose your words wisely. Students should be confident that you have their best interest at heart, always.

Assessments are a part of every classroom. Although we have made great strides in designing a variety of assessments, good old fashioned tests and quizzes are still abundant in most classrooms. If the purpose of an assessment is to evaluate if the student has learned the information, how you convey your feedback is paramount. Before you establish the routine of calculating the grade based upon the number of right answers in the context of 100 points, take some time to consider what other ways you can give valuable feedback to your students and cheer them on? You may opt to deliver a letter grade with detailed feedback on what they did right, as well as where they need improvement. You may want to highlight the incorrect information and allow students to make corrections before giving a final grade, or you may decide to embrace the concept of mastery learning, whereas students are given multiple assessments (not the same format or questions) to demonstrate mastery of the information before receiving a final grade. Whichever you choose, your role as your student's cheerleader should be evident. Your students should feel as though you are literally cheering them on to do well in their class, not playing the game of "gotcha" to see where their mistakes and flaws are.

Some teachers embrace the 9-5 business model of teaching. They come in, teach their classes and leave. They are very professional, they do a great job in the classroom and the administrative duties that are associated with teaching and when the dismissal bell rings, they leave. Now, there is nothing wrong with that model, and we have preached the importance of balance and self-care, but teachers who make an impact on students often go the extra mile and show up for their students at the extracurricular activities to cheer them on.

Whether it is a sporting event, school, play, fundraising activity or club, students want you there to support them. We know, the days are long! The last thing you may want to do is to extend your day by attending after school events, but trust us, it's worth it. The students and parents know who is in their corner. They recognize that you have sacrificed personal time to ensure that students are supported and loved. The bonus of attending these events is that behavior problems in the classroom seem to disappear. The establishment of positive relationships in and out of the classroom creates a strong foundation of trust and support for one another. Attending these events with family members strengthens the ties that lead to self-care and meaningful connections. Students want to support you, too!

COLLEAGUES

In every profession, there is some essence of competition amongst colleagues. Teachers are notorious for being altruistic, overachievers who want all students to like them the most. It's the ego that is hard at work. Because we are often a one-person show inside our classroom, we forget that we are part of the bigger team made up of our colleagues, administrators, and community members. Being a cheerleader for your colleagues demonstrates how secure you are in yourself. You're not in competition with the other third-grade teachers. You are part of a team. There is room for everyone to be a valued member of the school community. Make sure that you honor and celebrate your colleagues as much as you do your students. Every year, you get new students, but your colleagues are there to stay. Support them and love them.

I had a rule in my class: Never let students speak poorly of other teachers. Working in a high school, there was no shortage of students complaining about my colleagues. They would lament at how unfair the teacher was. The teacher didn't actually teach, they said something insulting etc. In the beginning of my career, I bought into some of these allegations, however, I quickly learned to see through it. Often, it was the student who wanted to avoid taking responsibility for their actions and used deflection as the method to draw attention away from themselves. When these situations arose in my classroom, I would immediately interject that I would not allow students to speak poorly of my colleagues in my classroom. I would also encourage them to conference with the teacher or their guidance counselor to find a resolution. In this way, I was supporting my colleagues. Now, with this being said, you cannot support immoral or unethical behavior. If you suspect anything inappropriate, reach out to your administrators to share your concerns. Your colleagues are not just the people that work in the same place that you do, they are an important part of your professional development.

Professional Learning Communities are not just made up of the teachers in your grade or department. They include all of the professionals in your school. Extend yourself by supporting one another, sharing resources and the workload, showing up for one another and cheering each other on. Work with your administrators to carve out time for colleagues to observe one another, share best practices, and collaborate. If you can't convince your administrators, utilize technology to connect with the staff in your school. Set up virtual meetings to brainstorm ideas, learn new skills, share resources, and solve workplace issues. We are stronger and better together.

Using social media to share articles about your students achievements, your school's events, and great success stories is a great way to strengthen the connection between school and home. It also resonates with community members. Proudly posting about your school and students says to others that you love your profession and your school community. That message goes wide and far. If you wish to keep your personal social media accounts private, consider creating a professional account that you use only for school related purposes.

We all have that friend that dresses from head to toe in gear for whatever holiday, sporting event, or theme is happening at school. Make no mistake about it; they exude enthusiasm for whatever the event happens to be. Wearing your school gear proudly has the same effect. It's a visual representation of you supporting your school and students. It's the perfect way to show school pride.

Having fun with your students and colleagues is a great way to show others that you are a cheerleader for your school and students. We have all read about passionate educators who do something outrageous like sleeping on the roof or shaving their head for a worthy cause. What they are doing is cheering on the teams or students to accomplish something really great. Make sure that you are part of the fun!

From the moment I walked into my classroom as a full-time teacher, I engaged in teaching and learning that was meaningful and fun. At the time, technology was beginning to enter the classroom. My digital skills were limited compared to some students, so I allowed them to teach me and the rest of the class. Common sense allowed me to realize that the students could facilitate some of the teaching and learning.

We learned their digital games and applied it to the curriculum (make sure you screen them first!) Paying attention to their passions initiated strong bonds. These relationships connected us to leadership qualities and service learning. We engaged in fundraisers to connect our class to the community, and we cheered each other on. Whether it was bowling for dollars or a talent show, we understood the power of team-building. Students would go above and beyond in the classroom to participate in our events.

Cheering on your students, staff, and school community is not just something that you do for them, it's also something that you do for yourself. Your experiences of participating in such activities connects you to the people who share the vision and mission of the school. You will be more invested in your school and students. So, let's go!

POINTS TO PONDER

- Who was your biggest cheerleader in your life?
- How did your cheerleaders demonstrate their support for you?
- How often do your students ask if you will come and watch them do something?
- Name the cheerleaders who show up and show out for your school. What qualities do they have that are contagious?

CHAPTER TEN

LEGACY

"What you leave behind is not what is engraved in stone monuments, but what is woven into the lives of others."
Pericles

Have you ever thought about what people are going to say about you in ten years? Twenty years? Thirty years? Even though your legacy continues, your best is yet to come.

What do you want your legacy to be? You will transmit your legacy by modeling who you are as a person and an educator. Your core values will speak to your students. Your passion will inspire passion in the people around you. As you build, students will know who you are.

F I always think about my legacy as my personal mission statement: Continually fine tune the quality of my life and the lives of the people around me through commitment and hard work while having fun.

As I live a life of service, one of my goals will always be to teach to the whole child. A key component of taking care of the whole child includes building relationships. One of my principals once told me, "Whether you are here for a day or decade, you will make a difference." My approach to life as an educator proceeded with that in mind.

When you decided to become a teacher, you probably never thought about your legacy but you had to decide on the type of teacher you wanted to become. Think back to why you became a teacher in the first place. It is a career where we can truly make a positive difference every single day. Approach your career with that mindset. As you become a master teacher, be cognizant that you are also becoming a great influencer. Your legacy starts the first day you arrive in your classroom and it continues long after you leave.

Personal development is a prelude to professional development. It can separate the great teachers and the great leaders from the good teachers and negative-influence leaders. *Fired Up Teachership* and *Fired Up Leadership* development includes your personal development. Your personal development begins at birth and ends at death. Your legacy goes beyond your existence in an organization. Your influence will have a chain reaction. Your students pass along your legacy.

Complacency should never be an option, especially when you include all stakeholders. Keep looking for better ways. Keep making connections. Keep your compass pointed to your core values. A critical piece of your legacy as an educator will be how you make people feel. Relationships continue to leave a profound impression. I cannot name one book I read in eighth grade but I can recite all forty-seven names of my classmates. You can probably name every teacher you had from kindergarten through graduate school. You can tell how every colleague and supervisor made you feel. Your students can, too.

If you are a teacher, people are talking about you. Be proactive. Give them something to talk about in a positive way. For instance, my teacher greeted me at the door. My teacher asked me about my pets. My teacher let me facilitate a lesson about baseball. A teacher asked me my name when I walked by their room; they made me feel important.

HOW DO YOU WANT PEOPLE TO TALK ABOUT YOU AT THE DINNER TABLE?

When students are given opportunities, they respond. Sometimes they need multiple opportunities. Your goal is not to be the favorite teacher but to be the teacher that loves your students. And if you are their favorite teacher, that's a bonus. You cannot create a perfect roadmap, but you can keep in mind that everyone wants to feel important because they are important. Extend these concepts to your colleagues, and it will become reciprocal.

One of your most satisfying experiences will occur when students come back to visit. Or when they send you a positive letter, email, social media shout out, and a plethora of other contacts. You will understand that you have been that conduit to a better life for your students.

FYour legacy as you become a *Fired Up Teacher* is a mindset. Would you want to be a student in your class? I drew upon the techniques of my favorite teachers. As my own children went to school, it gave me a new paradigm to view my own teaching style and commitment. Keep this in mind as you develop. Never become complacent.

When I was principal, we created a culture that gave everyone an opportunity for leadership including the students, and that is how they saw themselves. Leave a legacy of love and gratitude and start in your classroom. Get *fired up*!

When I became an administrator, I considered the principalship from all stakeholder angles. I truly believed that I was making a positive difference every day. There are many stories and positive contacts that I've had and continue to have with my students and former students. Look for the positives and oftentimes you find them. This validates that my career as an educator is my calling. These positives will validate yours, too. We need you!

I am blessed to have dozens of stories to share. One such story affirms that students never forget how you make people feel. I received an email from a student, her summation of her years in middle school. We modeled a culture and it became her mindset at an early age. It confirms that many years later she remains connected to experiences and behavior that she will pass on as part of her legacy.

I have more respect for the unsung heroes of our educational system. Like custodial staff, secretaries, and lunch room personnel. With this, you have shown us that much is the same in life and no one is any more or less important than anyone else. Everyone in our school practiced this and students were allowed to possess an inner light, and no one tried to stop the glow. School was so much a part of our lives, not only because we spent so much time there but because we enjoyed the time we spent. It's hard to get used to pep rallies that promote just sports instead of academic achievement, character, and leadership. I see now, while experiencing the diverse environment of high school, why you have to keep refining the one thing you can change - yourself. In closing, I love the quote, 'Can you hear with your heart?' because I truly believe that you can lead people to truth by love. Thanks for an awesome four years - the memories, the fun times, and most of all the character altering teachings on being a positive leader now and forever.

As part of a university leadership class, we used my last book, *Fired Up Leadership*. During the semester, we frequently talk about legacy. Because your legacy is a life-long process, the following is an excerpt from a university student that puts her life's legacy into perspective.

Reading this book and attending class has changed my perspective on life. Before my college experience, I did not expect much of myself. Now I understand that it is because one of my five domains was undiscovered. I had no passion. I did not understand my character or what I wanted to do in life. All I knew was I wanted to help people I just did not know how. It wasn't until I started committing to my education when I realized I can do anything I set my mind to. In the book, there is this saying, believe in yourself or no one else would.

Most people enter the profession of teaching soon after they graduate from college. They are often wide-eyed and bushy-tailed, and young. When we are young, we really don't put much thought into what our legacy will be. We are trying to carve out our place in the world. But so much of what you do early in your career starts to build your legacy.

Think of it like backwards planning. We know all about starting with the end in mind. Take some time and think about what you hope people will remember about you long after you have left the schoolhouse. What will they say? Will they think you were fair? Will they tell others that they knew you were in their corner? Will they describe you as a person with integrity? This book is about teaching, but your legacy is about the life that you will have led. Your legacy will be what you did for a living and what you did as a person.

When you stop and consider that your legacy is what you leave to others woven into their lives, you understand that you can be a change-maker. You will be a person of impact. My greatest hope is that I have impacted others in a positive way. I want them to know that I cheered them on every step of the way. I want my legacy to be someone who lived to serve others so that they could become the best version of themselves. I hope that the next generation of educators whose lives I have touched, pass the torch, and my legacy will live on for generations of educators to come. Like Frank, I have been so fortunate to have many years of teaching experiences and opportunity to create a legacy. When I began this wild journey, I knew I wanted to make an impact with students and colleagues. I may not have known exactly how, but I stayed true to my mission.

Recently I asked some of my previous students to reflect on my legacy to them. I was emotionally moved by their responses. I hope that someday you will know what your impact was to the lucky people whose lives you've touched.

You gave me your time and when no one else seemed to care and you stood by me all the way through my last days at school.

You made me feel loved, important, smart, valued, and funny as f*#k! You really had me thinking I could be a comedian!

Your legacy was that those students who couldn't learn, you taught.

Leaving your legacy behind is touching people's lives in ways you couldn't even comprehend. Leaving your legacy behind is leaving parts of yourself in others that you trust will carry on the messages you brought to them. People come into our lives at the points that we need them most. A lot of them end up being temporary, but someone like Mrs. Hill is someone who stays with you for life. She may meet her students in the classroom, but she continues teaching them forever.

I hope that everyone thinks about your legacy the way I do! Your legacy to me is the definition of what an educator should be. It's more than writing lesson plans, reading textbooks, and grading assignments. It's about teaching the student holistically. Teaching them about how to be a better person overall, not just teaching them the material from your class. Oftentimes teachers only tend to the students in their classes. You were the opposite. As I learn more about becoming a teacher, and aspiring to become an administrator, I know that I want to be this type of teacher. And when I become an administrator, I want my school building to be filled with teachers just like you. Teachers like you are a living testimony to what an educator should be, and I hope those who read this book, and hear this information, know that.

Just like all adults my age, I remember exactly where I was on September 11, 2001. A parent called to tell me to turn on the television in my office. The event changed the way we do everything.

The following year, when we were able to travel, we scheduled an eighth-grade trip to Washington, DC. The students were apprehensive about being searched and scanned when we entered the Holocaust Museum. The visit was compelling for a number of reasons. On the bottom floor there was a Childrens' Wall of Remembrance. It was made of tiles from all over the world with messages of hope.

We decided to do something similar in our school. In the main lobby, we started the Belhaven Renaissance Wall of Acceptance. As part of an assignment, every eighth grader was able to design a message of peace, hope, love, and acceptance. This became a tradition and a rite of passage when we revealed each section every year. People from all over the community would read every tile. Parents reveled in the character of their children. The wall has been copied by schools all over the world. Siblings would look for the tiles of older brothers and sisters. It was an opportunity for students to leave a positive message and that is what they did. These tiles included quotes and pictures that enabled students to be themselves and inspire the community.

Legacy is not what you leave behind physically, it's what you leave inside of people. It's how you touch their heart. That's how you touch their life. It's about being the light for others. We hope that you have an incredible career filled with countless stories of how you made a difference in the lives of others. We know that, if you keep being *fired up* about being a teacher everyday, you will have created a legacy of being a passionate educator who impacted countless lives. That is our wish for you. So, what are you waiting for? Go light the spark!

POINTS TO PONDER

- Who is the legendary person in your life that made a difference? Why?

- What do you hope people will remember about you as an educator?
- How will you ensure that your legacy lives long after you are gone?

CONCLUSION

"Starting strong is good, finishing strong is epic."
Robin Sharma

When we began writing this book our greatest hope was that we could impact educators like you to find ways that could keep you *fired up* as a passionate educator, and that you will go on to a long teaching career that fills you up the way our careers have filled us up. We want you to know what it is like to be a master teacher that impacts countless lives in positive ways. We want you to have the opportunity to create a legacy of love for your profession, your school and your students.

It all starts with you.

We can share all of our wisdom and experiences with you, but what you do after you finish this book is entirely up to you. Teachership is not a moment, it's a movement. It's the ability of a teacher to embrace the leader that lives within them without leaving teaching behind. It allows a passionate educator to have the best of both worlds by leading in and out of the classroom. The teacher-leader that you are, or will become, will profoundly impact your life and the lives of your students. The choice to become a teacher-leader begins with you.

Never forget why you got into the education business in the first place. Make your students and school community your north star and always look for the illuminating light of it when you get lost. It will bring you back to your "why" and remind you of what you need to be doing.

You are bound to go through different stages throughout your career, sometimes more than once, but hang in there. What's at the end of the rainbow is pretty fantastic! The master teacher has the awesome opportunity to make an impact on their schools, community, and their students. It doesn't get better than that!

So much of the success that you will have as a teacher, colleague, employee, leader, and stakeholder depends on relationships. Building positive relationships, with all those in your school community, will make everything easier. Trust us and trust yourself! Your ability to work together with your students, their families, your colleagues, and members of the administration in an intentional way that promotes equity and acceptance will curtail issues of discipline in the classroom, inequitable practices, miscommunication, isolation, and feeling overwhelmed. Make the time early on to develop great relationships with open lines of communication.

Ask any student and they can tell you who the teachers are that love what they do and those who are just putting in their time and collecting a paycheck. (The second group is the small minority of educators, but they exist.) How do they know which is which? It's obvious. Teachers who remain *fired up* give off positive energy that is palpable by everyone in the school community. They are walking cheerleaders for their school and their students. They are proud (and often loud, too) about the success of their schools and their students. They are committed to ensuring that every student feels welcome and can be a successful learner. They are helping to shape their students into good human beings that are confident leaders. They are creating a life-long legacy of being a change-maker and impacting lives. That's you! That's what *Fired Up Teachership* is all about.

Surround yourself with other passionate educators who are committed to making this profession the pinnacle of all other professions. You will be challenged in your role as a teacher and leader, but look for your north star and let it guide you back to your "why". Always come back. You've got some really important work to do—and your students are counting on you! Start telling your story. Start building your legacy. You are your future. Make it something to be proud of!

ABOUT THE AUTHOR

MICHELE RISPO HILL is a passionate educator who has dedicated a lifetime to the education profession as a teacher, author, and presenter of professional development. During her tenure in the classroom, Michele was honored as the teacher of the Year in 2014, she served on numerous committees, mentored new staff and was an advisor for the classes of 2009 and 2018 and the Jostens Renaissance program. Today, she serves as the Coordinator of Admissions and Strategic Marketing and Equity Specialist for a career and technical school in New Jersey.

Michele has developed and implemented professional development with a sharp focus on diversity, equity and inclusion, engaging students and educational leadership. Michele has authored numerous articles published in the area of education, as well as co-authored *100 No-nonsense Things that Teachers All Teachers Should Stop Doing*, and now is the co-author of *Fired Up Teachership*. Michele is a champion for students and staff; her enthusiasm and positive energy is contagious!

Michele completed her undergraduate studies at LaSalle University and then went on to acquire two master degrees — one from LaSalle in Bi-Lingual Studies and one from Wilmington University in School Leadership. She is the mother of four children: Zachary, Victoria, Julia and Jennifer, and the Nonni of 4 grandsons: Michael, Dean, Julian, and Vincent. Michele resides on Long Beach Island, New Jersey with her husband of over 35 years, John.

ABOUT THE AUTHOR

DR. FRANK RUDNESKY was the principal of Belhaven Middle School in Linwood, New Jersey for a span of two decades in addition to teaching at the high school and university levels. During that time, the school was recognized with numerous local, state, and national awards for leadership, technology influence, excellence in performance, and a positive culture. The school was often used as a visitation site for other educators from as far away as Japan.

Frank has developed, implemented, and studied leadership processes to enhance organizational culture. He has authored several books and numerous articles published in the areas of leadership and technology influence. Dr. R. resides in the Jostens Renaissance Educator Hall of Fame and sits on several non-profit boards including the New Jersey Schools to Watch core team.

Dr. Frank Rudnesky draws on his experience as an accomplished teacher, award-winning middle school principal, and transformational leader to deliver his captivating keynotes and presentations to hundreds of audiences. As you listen to Dr. R.'s style of storytelling and his unconventional journey in life, it will get you *fired up* to pursue your passion and empower others to find their passion. His engagement, enthusiasm, and positive energy are contagious.

Frank's education includes a BS from the University of San Francisco, an MBA from Rowan University, and a Doctorate from Widener University. He resides in Southern New Jersey with his wife, Dr. Kimberly, two daughters, Franki Maria, Danica Lyn, and their dogs, Maggie and Winnie.

CODE BREAKER INC

CONSULTING

To learn more about
MICHELE RISPO HILL AND
DR. FRANK RUDNESKY
or to book them for a visit to your school, district, or
event, visit www.codebreakeredu.com

Code
BREAKER

INSPIRE · INNOVATE

LEAD · TEACH · LEARN

CODE BREAKER LEADERSHIP SERIES

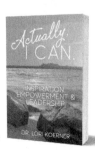

CODE BREAKER KID COLLECTION

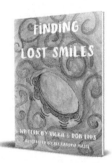

www.codebreakeredu.com